TEENS & the Supernatural & Paranormal

New Lenox
Public Library District
120 Veterans Parkway
New Lenox, Illinois 60451

HAL MARCOVITZ

THE GALLUP YOUTH SURVEY:
MAJOR ISSUES AND TRENDS

Teens and Alcohol

Teens and Career Choices

Teens and Cheating

Teens and Family Issues

Teens, Health, and Obesity

Teens and Homosexuality

Teens and the Media

Teens and Race

Teens and Relationships

Teens, Religion, and Values

Teens and Sex

Teens and Suicide

Teens and the
    Supernatural/Paranormal

Teens and Volunteerism

TEENS *& the* *Supernatural* *& Paranormal*

HAL MARCOVITZ

Produced by OTTN Publishing, Stockton, New Jersey

Mason Crest Publishers
370 Reed Road
Broomall, PA 19008
www.masoncrest.com

First printing

1 3 5 7 9 8 6 4 2

Library of Congress Cataloging-in-Publication Data

Marcovitz, Hal.
    Teens and the supernatural and paranormal / Hal Marcovitz.
        p. cm. — (The Gallup Youth Survey, major issues and trends)
    Includes bibliographical references and index.
    ISBN 1-59084-876-4
    1. Parapsychology—Juvenile literature. 2. Teenagers—Juvenile literature.
    I. Title. II. Series.
    BF1031.M346 2004
    130'.835—dc22
                                    2004013750

3 1984 00240 8019

Contents

Introduction

By George Gallup

As the United States moves into the new century, there is a vital need for insight into what it means to be a young person in America. Today's teenagers—the so-called "Y Generation"—will be the leaders and shapers of the 21st century. The future direction of the United States is being determined now in their hearts and minds and actions. Yet how much do we as a society know about this important segment of the U.S. populace who have the potential to lift our nation to new levels of achievement and social health?

The nation's teen population will top 30 million by the year 2006, the highest number since 1975. Most of these teens will grow up to be responsible citizens and leaders. But some youths face very long odds against reaching adulthood physically safe, behaviorally sound, and economically self-supporting. The challenges presented to society by the less fortunate youth are enormous. To help meet these challenges it is essential to have an accurate picture of the present status of teenagers.

The Gallup Youth Survey—the oldest continuing survey of teenagers—exists to help society meet its responsibility to youth, as well as to inform and guide our leaders by probing the social and economic attitudes and behaviors of young people. With theories abounding about the views, lifestyles, and values of adolescents, the Gallup Youth Survey, through regular scientific measurements of teens themselves, serves as a sort of reality check.

We need to hear more clearly the voices of young people, and to help them better articulate their fears and their hopes. Our youth have much to share with their elders—is the older generation really listening? Is it carefully monitoring the hopes and fears of teenagers today? Failure to do so could result in severe social consequences.

Surveys reveal that the image of teens in the United States today is a negative one. Teens are frequently maligned, misunderstood, or simply ignored by their elders. Yet two decades of the Gallup Youth Survey have provided ample evidence of the very special qualities of the nation's youngsters. In fact, if our society is less racist, less sexist, less polluted, and more peace loving, we can in considerable measure thank our young people, who have been on the leading edge on these issues.

And the younger generation is not geared to greed: survey after survey has shown that teens have a keen interest in helping those people, especially in their own communities, who are less fortunate than themselves.

Young people tell the Gallup Youth Survey that they are enthusiastic about helping others, and are willing to work for world peace and a healthy world. They feel positive about their schools and even more positive about their teachers. A large majority of American teenagers report that they are happy and excited about the future, feel very close to their families, are likely to marry, want to have children, are satisfied with their personal lives, and desire to reach the top of their chosen careers.

But young adults face many threats, so parents, guardians, and concerned adults must commit themselves to do everything possible to help tomorrow's parents, citizens, and leaders avoid or overcome risky behaviors so that they can move into the future with greater hope and understanding.

The Gallup Organization and the Gallup Youth Survey are enthusiastic about this partnership with Mason Crest Publishers. Through carefully and clearly written books on a variety of vital topics dealing with teens, Gallup Youth Survey statistics are presented in a way that gives new depth and meaning to the data. The focus of these books is a practical one—to provide readers with the statistics and solid information that they need to understand and to deal with each important topic.

* * *

If you have ever wondered about the attraction teens seem to have for the world of mystery and magic, and the possible effects of this attraction, you will find this book provides valuable information and insights that can point to appropriate parental responses.

The author examines specific groups such as Wiccans and Goths, provides historical background where it is available, and notes that fascination with the world of fantasy on the part of young people is nothing new. Discussion of the supernatural and the paranormal is interspersed with scientific explanations. Many other topics are covered, including angels and the recent intensified interest in End Times.

Reasons for the fascination of teens for the unseen world of magic and mystery are examined, as are the sometimes unhealthy and even tragic results of this fascination, as youth become desensitized or express their rage against society or life in general in violent ways.

Chapter One

Many people are interested in the supernatural and paranormal, and their interest is reflected in popular books, television shows, and movies like the 1999 blockbuster *The Sixth Sense*.

Scared Out of Their Senses

The novel *Eragon* tells the story of a 15-year-old farm boy who finds a blue egg that soon hatches into a dragon. Eragon and the dragon become friends and eventually embark on a mythical quest to avenge the murder of the boy's uncle. The two friends face many adventures together that involve magicians, elves, dwarves, and an evil tyrant. The book was an enormous success; by early 2004, *Eragon* was near the top of the bestseller list of the *New York Times*. More than 1 million copies were sold, mostly to an audience of young readers, and plans were made for a film adaptation of the novel.

The author of *Eragon,* Christopher Paolini, was just 15 years old when he wrote the book. It was an enormous achievement for a teenager to write a best-selling novel, particularly in the genre he chose: *fantasy* and the supernatural. Christopher's book hit the market at a time when popular culture has been saturated with books, movies, television shows, and video games that center on the supernatural and *paranormal*. For several years the most popular books for young people have been the novels in the Harry Potter series, which tell of the adventures of a young wizard in training. Among the most successful movies in recent years—both from a financial and critical standpoint—have been the Lord of the Rings trilogy, which tell about the adventures of heroes who battle a wicked sorcerer as they try to bring peace to the mythical land of Middle Earth.

There has never been a time when teenagers have not been fascinated by the supernatural and paranormal. In fact, most teenagers today may be shocked to learn that the novel *Frankenstein*, a frightening story that revolutionized the horror genre, was written by an 18-year-old girl. In the two centuries following the publication of *Frankenstein*, teenagers have become voracious readers of stories based on monsters, witches, wizards, ghosts, vampires, demons, dragons, devils, and aliens from outer space. They flock to horror, science fiction, and fantasy movies. Television shows such as *Buffy the Vampire Slayer* and *Charmed* have been among the most watched programs on the air, thanks to their large teenage audiences. Teens' tastes in the supernatural have influenced decisions involving hundreds of millions of dollars spent by book publishers, TV executives, movie producers, video game designers, and others who are anxious to deliver products that will give teenagers what they want.

"Courting and cultivating the lucrative youth market has been an important part of the work of the media industries for decades," wrote University of Colorado professor Lynn Schofield Clark in her book *From Angels to Aliens: Teenagers, the Media and the Supernatural.* "In recent years, however, the desire to appeal to teens has become even more intense. This is because today's teens represent the largest demographic group of young people ever—even surpassing their parents' generation, the baby boomers. A large amount of disposable income jingles in the 'echo boom's' pockets as they visit the malls, music stores, Internet sites, and theaters near their homes."

TEEN BELIEF IN THE SUPERNATURAL

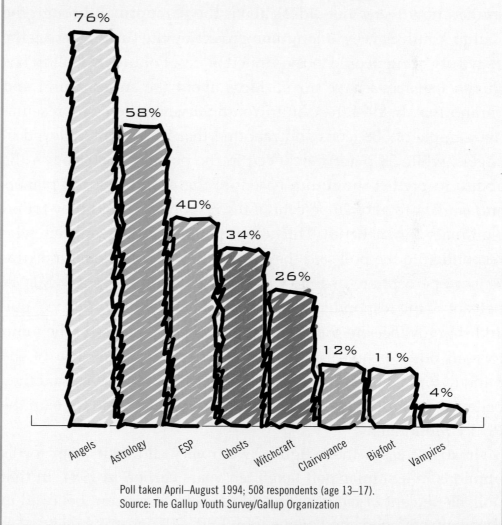

Poll taken April–August 1994; 508 respondents (age 13–17).
Source: The Gallup Youth Survey/Gallup Organization

But some people are concerned that constant exposure to stories about blood-suckers, grave-robbers, and flesh-eaters give teens anti-social ideas. Others believe that an interest in the occult or paranormal phenomena may prompt some of them to join *cults* or commit crimes.

Teen Witches

The Gallup Organization, a national polling firm, has often studied how teens view ideas about the paranormal through the Gallup Youth Survey, a longtime project by the firm to assess the views of young people in the United States. Polling by Gallup has shown that teens have mixed ideas about the supernatural and paranormal. In 1994 the Gallup Youth Survey polled a representative sample of 508 teens and reported that 76 percent believed in angels, while 58 percent believed in the power of astrology—the ability to predict the future based on the position of the planets and stars. A total of 26 percent of the respondents said they found legitimacy in witchcraft. Thirty-four percent of the teenagers who responded to the poll said they believed in ghosts. Belief in extrasensory perception, or ESP, was recorded at 40 percent, while 12 percent of the respondents said they believed in clairvoyance. ESP and clairvoyance are somewhat similar: ESP is the use of the mind to read other people's thoughts; clairvoyance is the use of the mind to foretell the future. Finally, 11 percent of the teens said they believed in stories about Bigfoot, a man-like beast said to roam the Rocky Mountains.

In many cases these figures were very different from teen's opinions in a similar poll taken ten years earlier, in 1984. In that poll, 69 percent of teens believed in angels; 55 percent believed in astrology; 59 percent believed in ESP; 20 percent believed in ghosts; 22 percent believed in witchcraft; 28 percent believed in clairvoyance; and 24 percent believed in Bigfoot.

The difference in the two studies indicates that over time the popularity of paranormal or supernatural phenomena fluctuate among teens. Interest in some of these ideas is undoubtedly affected by how they are portrayed in popular culture. For example, growing belief in witchcraft among teenage girls may have been influenced by recent portrayals of glamorous, seductive witches on television, in the movies, and in books.

Years ago, the best-known witch in the movies was the craggy, bent-over Wicked Witch of the West from the *Wizard of Oz*, played by character actress Margaret Hamilton. A 1985 Gallup Youth Survey reported that 100 percent of all teenage girls surveyed had seen the movie at least once. What girl would want to grow up to be a witch when the only role model available to her had green skin and died, rather ignobly, when a

During the 1990s, movies and television shows like the series *Charmed* made witches and witchcraft seem more attractive.

bucket of water was thrown in her face? But by the late 1990s witches had become more attractive, being portrayed on television by such actresses as Alyssa Milano (*Charmed*) and Melissa Joan Hart (*Sabrina: The Teenage Witch*). On the big screen Neve Campbell was featured in *The Craft*, a 1996 teen movie about witchcraft, while Nicole Kidman and Sandra Bullock starred as witches in the 1998 film *Practical Magic*. In recent years the New Age publishing company Llewellyn International enjoyed brisk sales of the book *Teen Witch*, selling more than 125,000 copies of the witchcraft manual, mostly to girls between the ages of 12 and 15. Von Braschler, Llewellyn's director of trade sales, told the *Bergen* (New Jersey) *Record*, "In places where witchcraft has not been hot, suddenly it's hot."

"It's not a fad. It's a social movement," is how Phyllis Curott explained girls' fascination with witchcraft to the *Bergen Record*. Curott, an Ivy League–educated lawyer, regards herself as a high priestess of Wicca, the name witches have given to their religion. Curott is also the author of *Book of Shadows*, the story of her journey into witchcraft. In an interview with the *Toronto Sun*, Currot commented, "There are lots of teenage girls and young women in the crowds at my book signings."

Teenagers from Outer Space

But from another perspective, when have witchcraft and other elements of the supernatural not been hot? According to the Internet site WorldwideBoxoffice.com, practically all of the 25 highest-grossing movies of all time have been based in the **genres** of horror, fantasy, or science fiction. The films on the list included the three Lord of the Rings films, five entries from the Star Wars saga, two movies based on the Harry Potter series of books, and assorted other fantastic stories like *ET: The Extra-Terrestrial* (1982), *Jurassic Park* (1993), *Independence Day* (1996), *Men in Black* (1997), and *The Sixth Sense* (1999). Chances are, similar films will soon be added to the list. In Hollywood, plans are underway to produce film versions of such classic fantasy stories as the Chronicles of Narnia series by C. S. Lewis as well as American author Edgar Rice Burroughs's series of books about Mars.

It should come as no surprise to any film fan that many of the movies on the top-grossing list include teenage or young adult characters central to the plots. In 1998 the media research firm ACNielsen EDI released a study of movie audiences that may help to explain why this is so. The firm determined that one-half of all people in the United States between the ages of 13 and 24 are "frequent or heavy"

Many of the most popular movies of all time have involved supernatural, paranormal, or extraterrestrial themes. One of these was *Independence Day*, in which aliens attack the earth.

filmgoers—a total audience in excess of some 20 million young people. The potential box office revenue from teenagers alone runs into the billions of dollars. "The motion picture industry has long struggled with accurately measuring the elusive teenage audience," said the ACNielsen study. "These frequent or heavy film-goers go to the movies at least once a month and drive a significant portion of all ticket sales."

Young people have been the focus of stories about the supernatural for decades. Motion pictures have been around for more

FRANKENSTEIN WAS A TEENAGER'S CREATION

It was supposed to be quiet summer on the shores of Lake Geneva in Switzerland, where the poet Percy Shelley and his new wife, 18-year-old Mary Wollstonecraft Shelley, had taken a villa. They shared their summer home with the poet Lord Byron and his girlfriend, Claire Clairmont. A fifth member of the party who joined them for the summer was a young physician, Dr. John Polidari. The year was 1816.

Country life didn't agree with the two young poets, who were more accustomed to wild times in Europe's lively capital cities. To break the boredom, Byron suggested a competition: everyone would write a ghost story. The others went about the task with relish, but Mary was troubled by the task and spent several evenings laboring to think of a story. Finally, she found inspiration while listening to her husband and Byron talk about a doctor who had apparently been able to make a dish of noodles wiggle as though they were alive. That night, Mary later wrote, she had a terrible dream in which she envisioned the story of a monster.

"Perhaps a corpse could be re-animated," Mary wrote. "Perhaps the component parts of a creature might be manufactured, brought together, and endowed with vital warmth . . . I saw the pale student of unhallowed arts than a century, but it was not until the 1950s that Hollywood movie studios started churning out films about teenagers. Some of the films were well-written and well-acted stories about real issues that faced young people, such as *The Blackboard Jungle* and *Rebel Without a Cause,* both released in 1955. On the other hand, many movies tapped into the horror and science fiction genres. Filmed on low budgets using unknown actors, the movies were produced with teenage audiences in mind. On a typical Saturday night at a drive-in movie during the 1950s, a boy and his date could enjoy a double-feature that might include such titles as *Teenagers from Outer Space* (1959), *I Was a Teenage Frankenstein*

kneeling beside the thing he had put together. I saw the hideous phantasm of a man stretched out, and then, on the working of some powerful engine, show signs of life, and stir with an uneasy, half vital motion. Frightful must it be; for supremely frightful would be the effect of any human endeavor to mock the stupendous mechanism of the Creator of the world."

And so was born the story of Frankenstein. Published three years later, the book tells of a scientist named Victor Frankenstein who stitches together a monster from parts of bodies he steals from tombs, then brings it to life. But things go wrong. The monster turns on Frankenstein and others until he is destroyed in a final showdown.

Nearly two centuries after *Frankenstein* was first published, the book remains in print. There have also been many movie versions of the story; the most famous is a 1931 movie starring the British actor Boris Karloff, who played the monster as a clumsy, erratic, and pitiful beast who enjoyed picking flowers with little girls and never understood why all but the most innocent found him so hideous.

(1957), or *I Was a Teenage Werewolf* (1957). In the werewolf film, young Michael Landon played a high-school student afflicted with **lycanthropy**, who carried out gruesome murders while wearing his varsity jacket.

The 1970s and 1980s introduced the era of the "slasher" genre: movies about homicidal madmen who go on killing sprees, mostly targeting teenagers. Three film series stand out from the period: the Friday the 13th movies, featuring a hockey mask-wearing killer named Jason Voorhees; the Halloween films, in which a similarly-masked madman named Michael Myers stalks teen victims; and the Nightmare on Elm Street movies, in which a demonic handyman named Freddy Krueger haunts young people in their dreams. The movies all had practically the same story. Usually, teenagers who misbehaved in some way, either by using drugs or alcohol or having sex, would find themselves murdered in graphic and cold-blooded fashion. Young characters who displayed responsibility or otherwise righteous behavior would miraculously be spared — although not without an end-of-the-film, nail-biting chase scene that finally concluded with the defeat of the stalker. And although the good teens survived, the stalkers generally did as well; after all, Jason, Michael, and Freddy were needed for the sequels.

Despite the thin story lines, graphic bloodletting, and wholly predictable endings, slasher movies struck a chord with young people. Pat Gill, a professor of media studies at the University of Illinois at Urbana-Champaign, said the genre proved to be immensely popular among young people because the films usually depicted aloof, uncaring parents who left their teenage sons and daughters on their own to deal with their troubles in their own ways. Gill, author of a research paper on the slasher genre, told her university's news bureau that most teens could identify with the characters in the films. Parents depicted in slasher films, she said, "are stupid, they are selfish, they don't listen, they don't seem to care about their kids. Or if they do care, they are unable to help their kids face the nightmares of the everyday world."

Carrie and Harry

The 1970s also saw the domination of the book industry by a horror writer from Maine named Stephen King. Writing mostly about the supernatural, King would become the most successful and prolific author of the era, churning out more than 40 novels and nearly 100 short stories as well as screenplays and nonfiction books. By 2004, 33 of his books had been adapted for release as theatrical movies, while 13 were adapted as TV movies or mini-series. Many of King's books and stories featured teenage characters confronted with the supernatural. His first novel, *Carrie* (1974), told the story of a lonely teenage girl with the power of telekinesis—the ability to move objects with her mind. Carrie spends most of the book being picked on and pushed around by school bullies while enduring life under the thumb of her domineering mother. At the end of the story, Carrie uses her power to lash out at her tormenters.

Although teenagers were undoubtedly reading his books and certainly going to the theaters to see the film versions of *Carrie* and other novels, King writes mostly for an adult market. During the 1990s a British writer named Joanne Kathleen Rowling began to write supernatural literature specifically for a younger audience. Before her first book, *Harry Potter and the Sorcerer's Stone* (1998), was printed, the publisher insisted that she go by her initials, J.K. Rowling, because the company feared teenage boys might not be interested in the book if they knew it had been written by a woman.

The success of the Harry Potter book series, about a young wizard and his friends, is a worldwide phenomenon. Here, young children in Paris grab copies of the French-language version of *Harry Potter and the Order of the Phoenix* in 2003.

The publisher's fears proved to be unfounded—*Sorcerer's Stone* and the next four books in the Harry Potter series set publishing industry sales records, totaling an astounding 250 million copies sold worldwide by early 2004. The Harry Potter books have been translated into 60 languages and sold in 200 countries around the world. Film versions of the first two books are among the most-watched movies ever, accounting for nearly $600 million in box office receipts.

In 2000, the Gallup Youth Survey asked 500 young people between the ages of 13 and 17 what they knew of the *Harry Potter* books. Sixty-three percent of the respondents said they were aware of the series, 32 percent said someone in their homes had read at least one of the Potter books, and 21 percent of the teens reported that they had read at least one of the books.

As millions of young people know, Harry Potter is a young wizard in training at the Hogwarts School of Witchcraft and Wizardry. An orphan, he started out in the first book at the age of 11, but Harry and the other students have been growing older in each successive book. In all the stories, Harry and his friends Ron and Hermione, also wizards in training, use all manner of spells and mystical powers to battle assorted evildoers.

Many young people are fiercely dedicated to Rowling's stories, and most have read each book several times. Greta Hagen-Richardson, a 12-year-old fan who lives in Chicago, Illinois, told *Time* magazine, "When I first read them, I thought, 'The characters really relate to you—they're kids. They have bullies and bad teachers.' It helped me understand something—people, maybe my friends, my teachers. It's influenced me to read more." And 9-year-old Tyler Watson, a devoted Potter reader who is suffering from leukemia, wrote in an essay submitted to Rowling's publisher, "Harry Potter helped me get through some really hard and scary times. I sometimes think of Harry Potter and me as being kind of alike. He was forced into situations he couldn't control and had to face an enemy that he didn't know if he could beat."

J. K. Rowling insists that her books tell more than just stories about magic and wizardry. She says there are morals to her stories. Harry, Ron, and Hermione learn important lessons. They mature. Rather than just snapping their fingers or waving magic wands, the young wizards use their minds to solve problems and help people. Why then, is it necessary to set the stories against a background of the supernatural?

The answer, according to Rowling, is that young people need to believe in magic. "There will always, always be books about magic, discovering secret powers, stuff that you're not allowed to do," Rowling told *Newsweek*. "It exists in adults, too. There's a small part of you that wishes you could alter external things to be the way they ought to be. One of the realities of growing up is realizing how limited your power is as an adult."

Chapter Two

Fascination with the occult is by no means a new concept. In the 1930s audiences marveled at Bela Lugosi's portrayal of Count Dracula in a series of vampire movies; long before that, *Dracula* and other gothic novels were popular among readers.

The Occult, Violence, and Mental Illness

For years, Rod Ferrell was consumed with the idea that he was a vampire. The teenager, who lived in a central Florida town near Orlando, told his friends that he had been born in the 15th century and had been a member of the privileged aristocracy of France. He sometimes went by the name Vesago, after a fictional vampire in a book written by Anne Rice. Ferrell often dressed entirely in black; he also dyed his hair black and let it grow long and painted his fingernails black as well. Despite the fact that the Orlando area enjoys some of the best weather in the country, Ferrell mostly stayed indoors, always with the curtains drawn, a habit that made him stand out even more. While many young people in the area sported year-round suntans, Ferrell's skin was always pale and pasty, which seemed to support his notion that he was a member of the undead.

In his room, Ferrell fashioned a small shrine that featured candles and burning *incense*. As a

16-year-old, Rod convinced some of his friends—including his 15-year-old girlfriend Heather Wendorf—to participate in unusual rituals before the shrine. Using razor blades, they would cut their bodies, then lick the blood from each other's wounds.

"It was really strange because back then, Rod was really my whole life," Heather told Aphrodite Jones, author of the book *The Embrace: A True Vampire Story*. "The whole vampire thing was my life at that point, because I didn't have other factors to go into. I didn't have an adolescent life. I wasn't social. I didn't have many friends. . . . My specialty was being a vampire."

On November 26, 1996, Heather's parents, Richard Wendorf and Naomi Queen, were killed after being struck numerous times with a tire iron. After Rod and three of his friends were arrested as suspects in the murders, a reporter tracked down Rod's grandfather, Harold Gibson. "They're saying Rod is a monster," Gibson said. "He's not a monster." Prosecutor David Harrington agreed, telling the Associated Press, "I think you had a group of kids that just wanted to be a part of something, wanted to belong to a group. And it went too far. Hopefully, it's over." Rod Ferrell ultimately received the death penalty for his part in the murders.

Sadly, this story is not unique. In recent years, there have been several cases of young people so consumed with the *occult* that they have lost touch with reality, often committing horrible acts. In one example, Kyle Hulbert, an 18-year-old self-described vampire from Maryland, pleaded guilty to killing a prominent scientist with a 27-inch sword. In that case, medical examiners counted 29 stab wounds in the body of the victim, nationally known biochemist Robert M. Schwartz. Hulbert told prosecutors that fellow vampires he identified as Ordog, Sabba, and Nicodemus had given him permission to commit the December 8, 2001, murder, and that an invisible dragon named Tiamet had accompanied him during the crime. "Everyone has a beast inside of them," Kyle told a reporter for WJLA news in Arlington, Virginia. "Everyone has . . . rage, anger, whatever. Mine might be a little closer to the surface than most."

Such cases are not confined to the United States. In Saxony, Germany, three teenagers committed suicide in August 2001 by jumping from a bridge. When police recovered the bodies, they found the teens wearing numerous symbols suggesting the boys had been involved in devil worship. "They were known as being involved in Satanism," prosecutor Dietmar Kipry told a reporter for the *Times* of London. "They went to parties in cemeteries and listened to the music of the [devil worship] scene." One of the boys left a note on the bridge. It read, "We are unhappy with this life and seek a better one." Police in Germany were particularly troubled by the suicides because it was not the first time teenage devil-worshippers had killed themselves. In the 12 months prior to the

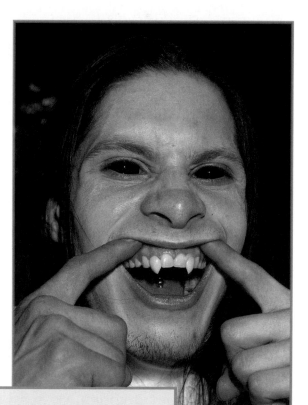

Some people become so obsessed with the occult that they may alter their appearance. In this case, a fan of vampires has had his teeth sharpened into fangs.

Saxony deaths, four other German youths had also taken their own lives. All of the teenagers were believed to be Satanists; one boy left a note that included the disturbing message "I give myself to Satan."

Innocent Fun?

Teenagers are inundated with stories about the occult, and many young people are enthusiastic recipients of that information. Do images of blood-sucking vampires, homicidal madmen, and devil-worshippers have the potential to lead young people into serious antisocial behavior? Many people would argue that the answer is no. For every Rod Ferrell there are millions of other young people who are able to watch movies about vampires or read books about demonic possession and accept the stories as nothing more than harmless entertainment. Clearly, Ferrell and Hulbert suffered from mental illnesses that caused the killers to lose touch with reality. It was their fascination with the occult that led them to take on the roles of mythical creatures.

Many movies and television shows—particularly those with occult themes—regularly include acts of murder and violence. This has prompted educators and mental health experts to wonder whether such grisly tales effect young people's minds. For example, consider the popular TV show *Charmed*, which tells the adventures of three young and attractive witches. "Scenes have included shots of bloody wounds, a decapitated head, bleeding eyes, and the nailing of a man's hand to a bar," indicates a viewers' guide issued by the California-based Parents Television Council (PTC). "In the season premier, the sisters vanquished one head of a two-headed demon, resulting in a charred and bloody stump. Deaths by burning, hanging, and electrocution are also shown." Another television show panned by the PTC is *Angel*, a spin-off of *Buffy the Vampire Slayer* that was cancelled in 2004. The organization named *Angel* to its list of 10 worst prime-time TV shows for the 2002–03 season because of its extremely violent and sexual content. "Despite its young target audience, *Angel* routinely features gory violence and graphic sexual encounters," wrote the PTC viewers' guide. "The series also sends a dangerous and irresponsible message to teenage fans by equating violence with sexual excitement. In many scenes, characters become aroused by fighting."

Over the past 30 years, there have been more than a thousand studies into the effects of violence in the media on young viewers. The vast majority of them have drawn the same conclusions: violent images in the media tend to cause violent and antisocial behavior by young people. The most common impact on young people who are exposed to constant media violence is that they become desensitized to what they see. They witness so many depictions of murders and mutilations on the screen, they don't recognize the true impact of such acts in the real world.

In 2002 the journal *Science* released a study that examined the effect of violent images on both adolescents and adults. The study followed the lives of 707 participants over a period of 17 years, tracking their viewing habits as children, teenagers, and adults. The *Science* study found that young people who watch more than an hour of television a day, regardless of content, are four times more likely to commit aggressive acts toward other people in their lives than those who watch less than one hour. In addition, after tracking the adolescent viewers into adulthood, the study found that nearly 29 percent of young people who watched more than three hours of TV a day were later involved in assaults, robberies, fights, and other aggressive behavior.

"[Children clearly] do become desensitized, they do copy what they see, and their values are shaped by it," commented Susan Villani, a psychiatrist from Baltimore. Dr. Michael Brody of the American Academy of Child and Adolescent Psychiatry agrees. "If television doesn't influence kids, then why are so many people spending so many billions of dollars to advertise?" he said in a *Christian Science Monitor* report on the issue. Although Brody did not feel television is the sole cause of violent behavior, he believed it certainly contributes to the problem: "Even if it represents 10 percent of the reason [for violence], somebody should look at this."

The Wrong Messages

Regulating what young people see on television or in the movies is not an area where lawmakers choose to tread too often. The First Amendment to the U.S. Constitution guarantees freedom of speech and expression, and over the years Congress has been very careful not to infringe on the First Amendment rights of writers and artists. Occasionally, though, laws are passed to clean up the airwaves. In 2004, Congress passed the Broadcast Decency Enforcement Act, which raised fines on broadcast companies from $27,500 per incident to a whopping $500,000 per incident when the Federal Communications Commission determines broadcasters violate its rules governing "obscene, indecent, or profane material."

The television, film, video game, and music industries have each taken some steps to keep young people from being exposed to violent or offensive material. In recent years all four media industries have voluntarily adopted parental advisory systems, which are supposed to warn parents when their products—be it a television show, movie, music CD, or video game—may contain graphic violent or sexual content.

The problem with the industry response is that if teenagers want to watch violent or sexually suggestive

The 2004 Broadcast Decency Enforcement Act increased fines on those who broadcast material deemed violent or obscene. Radio personality Howard Stern and others believe the law violates the First Amendment, and have argued that a clear legal definition of the term "indecency" is needed so that the law can be fairly applied.

TV, they can easily find a way. A 1999 report by the U.S. Senate Judiciary Committee found that 87 percent of all homes in the United States have more than one television set, and 50 percent of all American children have TV sets in their rooms. Also, the Judiciary Committee reported, nearly 89 percent of all American homes have video game equipment or personal computers. The panel's report added that the average teenager listens to some 10,500 hours of rock music between the 7th- and 12th-grade years. "By the age of 18, an American child will have seen 16,000 simulated murders and 200,000 acts of violence," the Senate report found. "Television alone is responsible for 10 percent of youth violence."

Over the years, the Gallup Youth Survey has gauged teens' reactions to sex and violence in the media. Results of the Gallup polls support the notion that teens are becoming desensitized to the images they see on television and movie screens. In 1977, the Gallup Youth Survey asked 502 young people between the ages of 13 and 17 whether they believe there is too much violence in the movies. Forty-two percent of the respondents answered yes. In 1999, the Gallup Youth Survey asked 502 American teens between the ages of 13 and 17 the same question. This time, just 23 percent of the respondents said they believed movies were too violent. During the intervening 22 years movies became arguably more violent, rather than less violent. There is a simple explanation for why teens in 1999 harbored a much more permissive attitude for what they were seeing in the movies: many of them simply could not discriminate between what is violent and what is not.

Teenage girls are more likely to believe images on the screen are too violent. The 1999 Gallup Youth Survey found that 26 percent of the girls and 20 percent of the boys feel there is too much violence in the movies, while 34 percent of the girls and 22 percent of the boys told the Gallup Organization that they feel there is too much sex in films or on television.

A similar Gallup Youth Survey suggested that while teens may have become desensitized to violence in the media, many young viewers nevertheless know that a steady dose of media violence is not good for them. In a 1998 Gallup Youth Survey of 500 young people between the ages of 13 and 17, 53 percent agreed with the statement "violence on television and in movies sends the wrong messages to young people." Although that survey reported that 31 percent of teens thought there is too much violence on TV and in the movies, the poll also offered further proof that young people were becoming desensitized to violence. According to the poll, 83 percent of the boys and 74 percent of the girls said they "do not have a problem watching violent movies or television programs." The data indicates that even though teenagers know movies and television programs are too violent—and even though they suspect what they're seeing is not good for them—they will watch anyway.

Dissociation from Reality

It is bad enough that young people can become bored or unfazed by media violence, but there is a vast difference between registering no emotion toward a murder committed on-screen and believing oneself to be part of the on-screen action. Indeed, while many young people may become desensitized toward what they see, very few will go to the next step and dissociate themselves from reality. An example of this condition is Lee Boyd Malvo, who during 2002 was involved in one of the most disturbing cases of serial murder in the nation's history. The 17-year-old and an older accomplice, John Allen Muhammad, were involved in the sniper slayings of 10 people in the Washington, D.C., area.

TEEN ATTITUDES CONCERNING VIOLENCE

Statement of attitude	Percentage who agree		
	All Teens	Boys	Girls
You do not have a problem watching violent movies or television programs	78%	83%	74%
Teens need a greater number of positive role models on television, in movies, and in song lyrics	72%	65%	79%
Movies and television have a great deal of influence on the messages to young people today	65%	60%	72%
Violence on television and in movies sends the wrong messages to young people	53%	44%	62%
There should be greater restrictions on the number and type of movies and television programs that include violence, sex, or bad language	43%	32%	55%
Watching violent television programs or movies makes teens violent	34%	29%	39%
Movies intended for teenagers contain too much violence	31%	26%	36%
Television programs intended for teenagers contain too much violence	29%	26%	32%

Poll taken 1998; 500 total respondents age 13–17.
Source: Gallup Youth Survey/The Gallup Organization.

During Malvo's murder trial, experts testified that the boy suffered from a dissociative disorder—a mental illness that caused him to lose touch with reality. Malvo's attorneys attempted to show that their client was not guilty by reason of insanity by suggesting he was obsessed with the science-fiction movie *The Matrix*. After watching the film more than 100 times in the months leading up to the murders, Malvo's lawyers claimed that the young man saw himself as the character Neo, who leads a small band of rebels against an evil society ruled by computers. The film depicts many violent gun battles between Neo and the forces of evil. What's more, experts testified, Malvo looked up to his older co-conspirator Muhammad as a mentor, much the same way Neo looks up to the character Morpheus.

The Matrix defense was a theory that prosecutors vehemently opposed. "How many million people have seen this movie and how many have committed murder?" asked prosecutor Robert F. Horan Jr. during an interview with the *Boston Globe*. In the end, the jury convicted Malvo for his role in the murders and sentenced him to life in prison.

Still, there is no question that Malvo had dissociated—his obsession with a supernatural theme had taken over his mind, prompting him to act out *The Matrix* scenario in real life. People who suffer from dissociative disorders lose connections to their memories, thoughts, and knowledge of what is right and wrong. Psychiatrists believe dissociating can provide the sufferer with a temporary escape from reality. Children who are abused physically and sexually have been known to dissociate as a way to protect themselves from the mental anguish of their experiences. As a child, Malvo may have experienced many traumatic incidents that could have led to his need to dissociate: evidence introduced at his trial suggested he had been beaten repeatedly by his mother. Even after Malvo and Muhammad were arrested, Malvo still continued to harbor delusions about himself. Sitting in his jail cell, social worker Carmeta Albarus testified, Malvo continued to believe he was Neo. "Mr. Malvo wanted me to know how unjust the society was and how important it was for them to build a new and just society," Albaraus testified during Malvo's trial. Also, attorneys produced sketches Malvo had made, drawing himself as Neo. Malvo wrote across one sketch, "The outside force has arrived, free yourself of the Matrix control."

Just because people dissociate doesn't mean they will become cold-blooded killers. Some people with dissociative disorders are able to function normally. Others could experience a number of mental and physical ills, including *depression*, mood swings, suicidal tendencies, insomnia, sleep walking, panic attacks, *phobias*, drug and alcohol abuse, eating disorders, *psychosis*, *hallucinations*, amnesia, trances, self-persecution, out of body experiences, and violence.

Kyle Hulbert and Rod Ferrell also had long histories of mental illness. Hulbert, who was sentenced to life in prison for killing Dr. Robert M. Schwartz with a sword, had been abandoned at the age of 7 by his parents. He spent most of the next 11 years of his life in and out of mental hospitals, during which time doctors had diagnosed him with *attention deficit disorder*, *bipolar disorder*, psychosis, and *schizophrenia*. Doctors said he was delusional and hallucinatory. "I can see dragons," he once told his friends, according to the *Washington City Paper*. He also told his friends that he was a vampire, and that his favorite movie was *Interview with the Vampire*, the 1994 film adaptation of an Anne Rice novel.

In Ferrell's case, doctors determined that the boy suffered from a persecution complex, believing that people wanted to harm him. Ferrell told psychiatrists that he truly believed he was a vampire, and could even smell people's blood. Psychiatrist Wade Meyers concluded that Ferrell was "on the fringe of not being in touch with reality" and that the teenager suffered from a schizotypal personality disorder. "People with a schizotypal personality disorder are very sensitive to stress, and when they are under stress, their personality can disintegrate," Dr. Meyers explained to prosecutors. "They are going to have less control over their judgment, less control over their behavior, less control over their emotions."

Ferrell told the doctor that he had been sexually abused as a child. Also, his home life had hardly been stable, and as a teenager he had been a heavy drinker and drug abuser. All those factors clearly pushed him toward the dangerous behavior that would finally manifest itself in the murders of Richard Wendorf and Naomi Queen.

But what about Ferrell's interest in the occult and his belief that he was the vampire Vesago? Was that the final factor that tipped Rod Ferrell over the edge? "I think it offered power and solutions to somebody who felt pretty powerless," said Dr. Meyers. "Rod was somebody who didn't have a whole lot of answers to life. He certainly didn't have a very good identity. He didn't feel good about himself. He didn't feel he could achieve very much in life. I think that gave him an alternative method to have some power, a way to feel good about himself."

Chapter Three

The distinctive "Goth" look is easy to spot at concerts and other public events. Studies indicate that a growing number of young people are attracted to the Goth lifestyle.

The Influence of the Occult

Falynn Trayer, a 17-year-old high school student from New York City, said she often needs a little extra help in school, so she calls on the power of the male and female *deities* worshipped in the Wicca religion. "I have no set rituals," she told a *New York Times* reporter. "If I want a better grade at school, I may ask the god and goddess for their help, burn a candle—something like that."

Wicca is heavily influenced by supernatural themes—its members cast spells, practice witchcraft, and believe in the powers of potions and black magic. It is one of many pagan religions, in which people look toward the supernatural for guidance and help in their personal lives.

Many young people who don't commit themselves to worshipping pagan or Wiccan deities still seek a lifestyle oriented toward the occult. They are known as Goths and can be recognized mostly by their fondness for black clothes, body piercings and tattoos, black fingernail polish, and devotion to the dark lyrics and angry music of such pop music stars as Marilyn Manson, Rob Zombie, Slayer, and Evanescence. Goths consider themselves outcasts from society and bond with each other through their lifestyles on the fringe. Many Goths harbor a fascination for violence, death, drug use, and self-mutilation.

Still deeper in the underbelly of society are said to lurk the Satanists. Their supposed strange and obscene rituals have horrified tabloid newspaper readers and movie fans for decades. However, a considerable amount of evidence suggests that devil worship is much-publicized yet little-practiced in the United States. It appears that the few people who actually practice devil worship do so as individuals or as members of very small, loose-knit groups.

Falynn Trayer observes the rituals of Wicca in a large city proud of its diversity and tolerance of alternative lifestyles. But a lifestyle influenced by the occult can be lived anywhere in the United States—even amid the cornfields and conservative culture of Middle America. Just ask Cat Spiker, 19, who lives in the Quad-Cities area of Iowa and considers herself a Goth. "The world is evolving and people are looking for other ways to experience life," Cat told a reporter for the *Quad-Cities Times*.

As teenagers grow older and are exposed to different cultures and lifestyles, some young people are drawn to groups associated with witchcraft and the occult. Evidence suggests that membership in such groups is growing.

Obsession with Death

The original Goths were a Germanic people who settled north of the Black Sea in the third and fourth centuries. Researchers don't know much about the early history of the Goths, but one theory suggests they migrated from Gotland, an island near Sweden in the

Baltic Sea. Whatever their origins, the Goths were feared by their enemies because they sacrificed their captives to their gods of war. Goths were regarded as barbarians—brutal, uncivilized killers.

It is more likely that modern Goths have based the name for their movement on the word *gothic*, which is used to describe the art and architecture common during the Middle Ages. Gothic style, which dominated architecture in Europe from the 12th through 16th centuries, features an abundance of stone arches, tall columns, pointy spires, and thick walls. A textbook example of gothic architecture is the Cathedral of Notre Dame in Paris. Modern Goths are probably less interested in the origins of the architecture than in the type of mood it conveys: dark, mysterious, somber, and dangerous—like the atmosphere of Dracula's castle or the setting for an Edgar Allan Poe story.

Contemporary Goth culture first surfaced in Great Britain during the early 1980s at a London bar named the Batcave. Early Goth fans listened to such musical groups as Alice Cooper, Black Sabbath, and Siouxie and the Banshees. In the United States, Goths could be found at art movie houses, attending midnight screenings of cult film classics such as *Cabinet of Dr. Caligari* and *Nosferatu*—movies made during the silent era that captured the look and feel of contemporary Goth culture. More recently, pop stars like Marilyn Manson and Rob Zombie have replaced Alice Cooper and Ozzy Osbourne, and Hollywood has responded to Goth tastes with such films as *The Crow* and *House of 1,000 Corpses.*

Goths remain tied to absolutely no groups, other than perhaps small circles of friends who may share a similar fascination with the supernatural and an obsession with death. David Hart, a Christian youth minister from Pittsburgh, reaches out to Goths by dressing in black and visiting nightclubs and similar places where

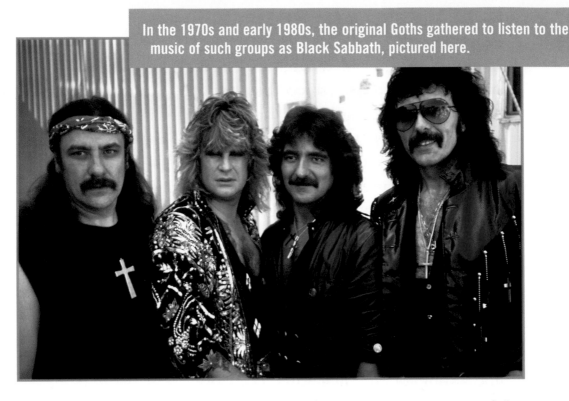

In the 1970s and early 1980s, the original Goths gathered to listen to the music of such groups as Black Sabbath, pictured here.

they congregate. He tries to convince them to give up some of the riskier habits they practice, such as sipping each other's blood, which can enhance the spread of Acquired Immune Deficiency Syndrome, or AIDS. "These kids romanticize death," Hart told a reporter for the *Pittsburgh Post-Gazette*. "They romanticize the blade, the blood that trickles down. They write very, very sad introspective, self absorbed poetry."

Source of Life

Wiccans are not obsessed with death; instead, they worship the Earth and believe the planet is the source of all life. Wiccans regard themselves as members of a legitimate religion and the U.S. government has agreed with them. In 1997, the U.S. Army recognized Wicca as a religion and gave instructions to army chaplains in how to lead services for Wiccan soldiers. "Most Wiccans meet with a coven, a small group of people," the army's handbook for chaplains says. "Each coven is autonomous. Most are headed by a High Priestess, often with the assistance of a High Priest . . . Most covens are small. Thirteen is the traditional maximum number of members, although not an absolute limit. At that size, covens form a close bond, so Wiccans in the military are likely to maintain a strong affiliation with their covens back home."

A coven of Wiccans will typically meet to celebrate the seasons and cycles of the moon. On full moons a Wicca priestess will lift a dagger over a ball of salt in a rite that Wiccans say honors the Earth. Wiccans celebrate eight holidays a year, most of which correspond with the change of seasons and similar events, such as April 30, which is known as Beltane or May Eve, and January 31, which is Oimelc or February Eve. "[Wicca is] nature based and follows the seasons," Oklahoma Wiccan Riche Bright explained in a newspaper interview. "We believe in the god and goddess rather than just one God. We believe there's good and evil in everybody and everything."

There is no question, though, that elements of witchcraft, such as the casting of spells, are very much a part of the

The pentacle, or pentagram, is one of the most popular and powerful symbols used by Wiccans and followers of other pagan religions.

Wicca movement. Such staples of the occult as *Tarot cards*, magic wands, and ceremonial *chalices* are typically employed during Wicca rites. Many Wiccans wear a symbol known as a pentacle — a five-pointed star that points up. The pentacle represents the four elements of earth, air, fire and water; the fifth element represented in the star is the spirit possessed by the wearer.

The American Religious Identification Survey, a project conducted by City University of New York, estimated in 2001 that 134,000 people living in the United States consider themselves Wiccans. Since just 8,000 people were thought to be Wiccans in 1990, the study concluded that Wicca may be the fastest growing religious movement in the United States. In addition, the study reported that 140,000 people living in the United States identify themselves as members of other pagan religions.

Despite the growing numbers, there is no national organization of Wiccans led by a single, supreme priest, priestess, or witch; nor is there an effective national organization of pagans.

History of Witchcraft

Witchcraft has a long history dating back to *medieval* times. Mostly, it has been regarded as a threat to Christianity and witches have been hunted down and persecuted, often falsely. In Europe, witches were arrested, tortured, and executed during the *Inquisition*. The Puritans of Salem, Massachusetts, led by the minister Cotton Mather, staged witchcraft trials that remain one of the darkest chapters in America's history. The trials resulted in the hangings of 20 men and women, many of whom were falsely accused.

Nevertheless, the legends, rituals, and foundations for modern witchcraft survived the witch hunts; these were revived in 1954 by a British civil servant and devotee of witchcraft named

Gerald Gardner, who wrote a book titled *Witchcraft Today*. Gardner's work is regarded as the spark that ignited the modern Wicca movement. He combined elements of *folklore*, magic, and occult rituals, but underneath it all was a deep appreciation for life and the spiritual strength Wiccans believe they can draw from the Earth. "Rather than a separation of life and spirit, it's a

A Tarot reader spreads out her cards. The history of Tarot cards is believed to date back to ancient Egypt, although the cards also use symbols from the Greek and Roman civilizations. Today, Tarot reading is an important aspect of Wicca.

life-affirming religion," explains Wicca priestess Laura Smith. She and her husband Tony founded an organization of Wiccans in Norman, Oklahoma, that meets regularly in a Unitarian church. Membership has steadily increased since the group started in 1990. "Instead of having to hide in the broom closet, these [meetings] were out in the open and in public," says Laura Smith. "People started coming and it grew. It has thrived."

Other pagans trace the roots of their religions much further back. Pagans have based elements of their faith on the beliefs of the ancient Norse, German, and Anglo-Saxon peoples, dating back more than 2,000 years. Like the Wiccans, they believe in multiple deities and harbor a deep appreciation for the Earth and its powers. "A Pagan religion . . . resembles a tree," says the World Wide Web site of the Universal Federation of Pagans. "It emerges from the Earth, grows, changes, bears flowers [and] fruit, and shares its life with other living creatures. It is not made, it becomes. When its time ends, it does not pass from this world, for its 'children' have, in the interim, sprung up from the Earth, each similar yet unique. A world of pagan religions is like a forest: Natural!"

Pagans also look to the supernatural for guidance, relying on magic spells, occult rituals and the concoction of potions to see them through various crises in their lives, such as troubles with their love lives as well as troubles with their math homework. Need help mending a broken heart? A visitor to the Internet site www.Witchway.net would find, under a link to "Pagan Spells and Rituals," instructions to gather such ingredients as apple-blossom, peach and strawberry oils, strawberry leaves, strawberry tea, pink candles, salt from the sea, a wand carved from the branch of a willow tree, mirror, copper penny, crystal bowl, and various roots and herbs, such as jasmine and yarrow. Once all the ingredients are gathered, the lovesick pagan is instructed to follow this ritual:

> On a Friday morning or evening [the day sacred to Venus] take a bath in sea salt in the light of a pink candle. As you dry off and dress, sip the strawberry tea. Use a dab of strawberry oil as perfume or cologne. Apply makeup to groom yourself to look your best. Cast a circle with the willow wand around a table with the other ingredients. Light the second pink candle. Mix all oils and herbs in the bowl. While you stir look at yourself in the mirror and say aloud: 'Oh, Great Mother Goddess, enclose me in your loving arms and nurture and bring forth the Goddess within me.' Gaze deeply into the mirror after you have finished mixing the ingredients and say aloud, 'I represent the Great Goddess, Mother of all things. I shine in the light of the Golden Wings of Isis. All that is great and loving only belongs to me.' Then put half the mixture in the pink bag and add the penny and crystal. Carry it with you always [or until you find another love]. Leave the other half of the potion in the bowl, out in a room where you will smell the fragrance. Repeat this ritual every Friday if necessary.

Like Wiccans, pagan groups are very loosely organized. Over the years, there have been attempts to unite pagans into a national and even worldwide organization, but those efforts have had

questionable results. In 1991, for example, several pagan groups agreed to establish the Universal Federation. The group was incorporated and a headquarters established in Georgia. On its Web site, the Universal Federation boasts that "there are thousands of active congregations [covens, groves, temples] throughout the British Isles, the United States, Canada, Brazil, Australia, Germany, Denmark, Finland, Sweden, France, Italy, Spain and even Russia."

However, the organization is also quick to add that there is really no organization to paganism. "There is no central authority or doctrine binding on all congregations, and individual groups vary," the federation's Web site says.

Wiccans and pagans believe their faiths are misunderstood; that the media places too much emphasis on the supernatural aspects of their movements, and that many people believe they are devil-worshippers. "There's such a stigma attached to [Wicca] because in Oklahoma, 'witch' tends to equal 'Satanist,'" said Riche Bright. Added Wiccan Craig Corman, "We get frustrated by the stereotypes that Hollywood puts on us. We are loving, spiritual people. Hollywood often misconstrues religious genres for the sake of making a buck." Still, there is no getting around the fact that both religions have their supernatural overtones. When 12-year-old New York Wiccan Ashley Musto was asked by a reporter for PBS whether she practices witchcraft, she answered: "You have a spell that could help you with anything you could be worrying about, anything on your mind. If you need to talk to someone, you could pray to a spirit. It's just really, really helpful."

Protests from the Mainstream

Wiccans and pagans have their opponents, mostly conservative Christian groups and political leaders who question whether Wicca and paganism are truly legitimate religions. Some of these critics have even taken issue with the Harry Potter books, claiming that they promote witchcraft. In an essay published by *Christianity Today*, Wisconsin teenager Jacqui Komschlies wrote, "Author J.K. Rowling admits some *Harry Potter* readers have convinced themselves that Harry's world is real. Rowling has said she gets letters all the time, desperate letters addressed to Hogwarts, begging to be allowed to attend Harry's school. When fantasy produces that kind of reaction, we are naïve to assume that witchcraft is merely a harmless, fun literary device."

Marcia Montenegro, a former astrologer who founded the group Christian Answers for the New Age, told a reporter for PBS, "Christians definitely ought to be aware that witchcraft is very appealing to teenagers. A lot of teenagers today are actually targeted by the publishers of occult books. Web sites also will have information for teenagers and encourage their interest."

The U.S. Army's acceptance of Wicca rankled conservative political leaders. In 1999, a Texas newspaper published a feature on a Wicca religious ceremony at Ford Hood. The newspaper's coverage of the event included photographs of shirtless soldiers celebrating a

Wicca Spring Rite ceremony by leaping over a campfire, while women priestesses dressed in robes presided over the ceremony. The story sparked intense protests by Christian groups. "Please stop this nonsense now," U.S. Representative Robert L. Barr Jr. of Georgia wrote to the commanding officer of Fort Hood. "What's next? Will armored divisions be forced to travel with sacrificial animals for Satanic rituals?" Despite the pressure, the army insisted that Wiccan soldiers have a right to practice their faith. Since then, Wicca circles have openly observed their rituals at army posts in Louisiana, Alaska, Florida, and the island of Okinawa near Japan.

Even the White House has taken a position on paganism. In November 2003, H. James Towey, President George W. Bush's director of faith-based and community initiatives, questioned whether pagans perform charitable work, a duty many religious leaders believe is sacred and an important role for members of their faiths. "I haven't run into a Pagan faith-based group yet, much less a Pagan group that cares for the poor," Towey insisted in an on-line forum. Towey was quickly corrected by Pagan leaders, who pointed out that members of their faith support a battered women's shelter in Chicago and have raised money for AIDS victims in Massachusetts and homeless people in California.

Occasionally, pagans and Wiccans have fought back. In 2003, the parents of 14-year-old India Tracy of Maynardville, Tennessee, sued the Union County school system, claiming their daughter had to endure harassment because of her pagan beliefs. The lawsuit said India was punished because she refused to portray the Virgin Mary during a Christmas play and for refusing to attend a Christian worship service during school hours. "The last straw was when India was chased down the hallway by three boys who grabbed her by the back of the neck and told her she should change her religion

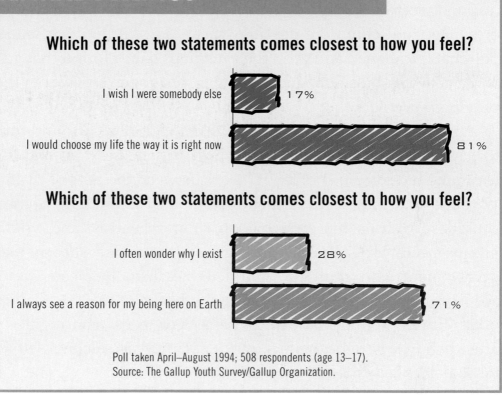

Which of these two statements comes closest to how you feel?

I wish I were somebody else — 17%

I would choose my life the way it is right now — 81%

Which of these two statements comes closest to how you feel?

I often wonder why I exist — 28%

I always see a reason for my being here on Earth — 71%

Poll taken April–August 1994; 508 respondents (age 13–17).
Source: The Gallup Youth Survey/Gallup Organization.

or they'd change it for her," India's mother, Sarajane Tracy, told an Associated Press reporter. India added, "What we are isn't on TV; it's totally different. Nobody listened. They just said I was wrong, that we were wrong, and that we were going to go to hell."

Opponents to Wicca and paganism may be overreacting. For starters, even though the City University of New York study identified Wicca as the fastest-growing religious movement in the United States, it is important to realize that Wiccans make up less than one-tenth of 1 percent of the 159 million Americans who claim membership in a religious organization.

According to the Gallup Youth Survey, the majority of young people today are maintaining their commitments to traditional religions, even more so than adults. In 2003, 43 percent of the respondents to a Gallup Youth Survey said they attended a church or synagogue within the previous seven days. A similar Gallup poll that questioned adults on their religious habits found that just 38 percent of adults attended church or synagogue services in the previous seven days.

A separate Gallup Youth Survey taken in 2003 also found that teenagers do more at church than simply attend services and listen to the sermon. The poll of 517 teens between the ages of 13 and 17 found that 30 percent of them participated in church-oriented activities, such as religious school, choir rehearsal, and youth group meetings. Gallup Youth Surveys have also shown that involvement with church-related activities usually means teens are less likely to experiment with risky behavior. A 2003 Gallup Youth Survey found that just 24 percent of teens who regularly attend church or synagogue services say they use alcohol, while just 6 percent say they have used tobacco products.

Truth and Myths About Satanism

Modern depictions of the devil as a horned red creature with a tail largely evolved in popular culture through the work of such classical authors as the English writer John Milton, whose poem *Paradise Lost* envisioned the devil as a fallen angel, and the Italian poet Dante Alighieri, whose *Divine Comedy* described an underworld in which the souls of sinners are damned to eternal suffering. During a tour of hell, Dante found the souls of sinners enduring icy winds, struggling under the weight of heavy rocks, boiling in rivers of blood, burning on hot sands, and frozen up to their necks in a deep, dark pit.

Teens believe such a place awaits sinners in the underworld. In a 1991 Gallup Youth Survey, 76 percent of teens said there is a hell where wicked people are punished. (Heaven received an even higher vote; 91 percent of young people told the Gallup Youth Survey that good people are rewarded in heaven.)

Many people also believe that there are hidden cults of devil worshippers living in the United States. However, most people who have studied this issue say that although there are some individuals or a small groups who practice the strange rituals of Satanic worship, there is no widespread organization of Satanists. In 1992, the Federal Bureau of Investigation (FBI) conducted a thorough

This drawing from an edition of John Milton's epic poem *Paradise Lost* shows Satan being cast out of heaven.

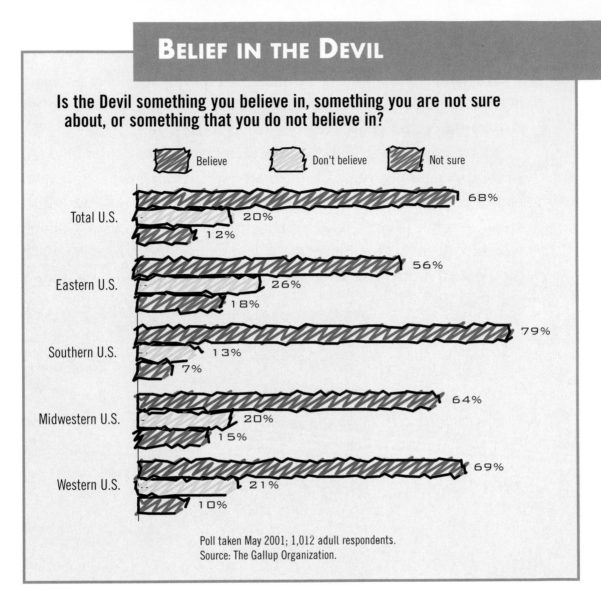

BELIEF IN THE DEVIL

Is the Devil something you believe in, something you are not sure about, or something that you do not believe in?

Believe | Don't believe | Not sure

Total U.S.
- 68%
- 20%
- 12%

Eastern U.S.
- 56%
- 26%
- 18%

Southern U.S.
- 79%
- 13%
- 7%

Midwestern U.S.
- 64%
- 20%
- 15%

Western U.S.
- 69%
- 21%
- 10%

Poll taken May 2001; 1,012 adull respondents.
Source: The Gallup Organization.

investigation of Satanism. After sifting through some 12,000 allegations of illegal activity involving devil worshippers, the bureau concluded that there is no evidence that a widespread Satanic movement exists in the United States.

The media helps to promote the idea that Satan-worship is widespread. Newspapers and magazines occasionally report on instances in which people are suspected of involvement in Satanic rituals, and Hollywood has explored the issue with such popular films as *Rosemary's Baby* (1968), *The Devil's Advocate* (1997), and *Fallen* (1998). In 2003 attorneys for accused killer Scott Peterson, who was charged by California authorities with the murder of his wife Laci and their unborn child, briefly suggested that the victims had actually been killed by a cult of Satan worshippers—a claim that was disregarded by experts for lack of evidence.

Over the years, people who claim to have been victims of Satanic cults have published biographies in which they describe how they were drawn into a life of bizarre sexual practices, torture, human and animal sacrifices, and contact with supernatural beings—including, perhaps, the devil himself. Among those stories are *Michelle Remembers*, written in 1980 by Michelle Smith and her psychiatrist and husband, Laurence Pazder. Here is how Michelle Smith described her vision of Satan, "He always came out of the fire, and his shape was constantly changing. You never saw a whole person at once—just a huge gigantic foot or a long, hairy leg." However, critics of Smith's book remain skeptical, arguing that few witnesses have stepped forward to corroborate Smith's story. Likewise, few of the stories of Satanism recounted by others have been corroborated.

"In the late '80s and early '90s, there was something called the 'Satanic Panic' in which there were a number of allegations about Satanic cult activities—ritual sacrifices, abductions, slayings," says New Jersey–based cult expert Rick Ross. "When the FBI looked into it and numerous law enforcement agencies looked into it, they found nothing. And so [Satanism] became kind of an urban myth. There is really nothing to substantiate that there are roving cults in California or elsewhere in the country that subscribe to Satanism."

Chapter Four

The Muslim shrine known as the Dome of the Rock rises over the remains of the Jewish temple in Jerusalem. The temple was destroyed in A.D. 70, but many Christians believe the world will end after it is rebuilt.

End Times

In 1948, an event unfolded in the Middle East that captured the attention of *evangelical* Christians in the United States and elsewhere: the state of Israel declared itself independent. The establishment of the Jewish state touched off a war between Israel and the neighboring Arab nations, and set the stage for decades of unrest and bitter relations that continue to exist in the Middle East today. Over the years the conflict between Jews and Muslims has affected the lives of millions of people touched by international terrorism, the price and availability of oil supplies, and even the balance of power between the United States and the former Soviet Union.

And yet, evangelical Christians found themselves interested in events in the Middle East for far different reasons. In several books of the Bible, it is prophesized that Jesus Christ will not return to Earth until the Jews reestablish their homeland in Israel. Luke 21: 29–31 says, "Look at the fig tree and all the trees. When they sprout leaves, you can see for yourselves and know that summer is near. Even so, when you see these things happening, you know that the kingdom of God is near."

Biblical scholars believe the "fig tree" in that passage refers to the state of Israel, and that the "leaves" sprouted in 1948 when the Jews took control over their ancient homeland. For centuries evangelical Christians have expected the return of Christ, but with the emergence of the state of Israel many Christians came to believe the world is truly headed for the era known as the End Times.

Evangelical Christians believe the End Times, or End of Days, will begin with the Rapture—an event during which Christ calls all true believers to heaven, leaving nonbelievers behind. The Rapture will be followed by a seven-year period known as the Tribulation, during which there will be wars and catastrophic events like earthquakes, floods, and meteor strikes. According to biblical *prophecies*, there will be plagues and fires, and locusts, scorpions, and other creatures will invade cities. A third of the remaining world population will die. At the conclusion of the Tribulation, God will defeat Satan, also known as the Antichrist, who will be imprisoned for 1,000 years while the world enjoys a period of peace.

Following the return of the Jews to their homeland, Christian scholars, ministers, and others have observed other world events and, when comparing them to the prophecies of the Bible, concluded that the current era of life on Earth may be occurring on the eve of the *Apocalypse*. For example, Matthew 24: 6 says, "And you will be hearing of wars and rumors of wars; see that you are not frightened, for those things must take place, but that is not yet the end." Certainly, wars have been common throughout human history; now, with the availability of 24-hour TV news channels and the Internet, it is impossible for most people not to be aware of them.

Matthew 24: 11 says, "And many false prophets will arise, and will mislead many." In 1993, 86 members of the Branch Davidian cult died in a shootout and fire at their compound in Waco, Texas, after they refused to surrender to federal agents. Among the dead was their leader, David Koresh. A similar cult was the so-called People's Temple, which tried to carve out a utopian society in the jungles of Guyana in South America in the late 1970s. The group was led by a flamboyant minister from California named Jim Jones. When Jones ordered cult members to commit mass suicide; some 900 complied. Koresh and Jones can be described as false prophets, who took on godlike prominence among their followers before leading them into tragic consequences.

Revelation 9: 16 says, "And the number of the armies of the horsemen was two hundred million; I heard the number of them." The first army to number 200 million is the army of

Cult leader David Koresh, along with many of his followers, died when the Branch Davidian compound in Waco, Texas, was destroyed after a 51-day standoff with the FBI in April 1993.

communist China, certainly a nation that has not accepted the Christian God as its savior.

And Timothy 3: 1 says, "But realize this, that in the last days difficult times will come. For men will be lovers of self, lovers of money, boastful, arrogant, disobedient to their parents, ungrateful, unholy, unloving, unforgiving . . ." Christians in search of examples of "lovers of self, lovers of money" need look no further than the executives caught up in the corporate scandals in the early years of the 2000 decade.

The Final Conflict

In the United States today, young people do not have to sit in churches to be exposed to discussion of the End Times. They can read the enormously successful books in the *Left Behind* series to follow the adventures of a group of Christians as they survive the Tribulation and await the defeat of the Antichrist. There is even a *Left Behind: The Kids* series for young readers. The books have proven to be enormously successful in the youth and adult fiction markets, selling more than 60 million copes since they first hit the store shelves in 1995.

Early in the first *Left Behind: The Kids* book, titled *The Vanishings*, 16-year-old runaway Judd Thompson Jr. wants to get as far away from his parents as possible, so he scrounges some money and buys an airline ticket for London. But on the trip across the Atlantic Ocean, Judd begins noticing unusual events on the airplane—passengers start disappearing. And not only do they vanish, but they leave behind their money, their luggage, their clothes—even the fillings from their teeth. Judd wants to talk about what he is seeing with the passenger in the next seat, a large man who boarded the plane with Judd back in Chicago. Suddenly, though, Judd discovers the man is missing, too.

Judd is one of four teenage characters whose stories are followed throughout the *Left Behind: The Kids* novels. Readers soon learn that Judd and the other teenagers are in for some rough times. The Rapture has occurred, and those who have been left behind must fend for themselves during the seven-year period before the Battle of Armageddon, the catastrophic and final conflict between the forces of good and evil. The *Left Behind* teenagers find themselves virtually alone as they try to survive horrific and bloody battles, terrible acts of nature, and supernatural events all orchestrated by Satan.

Jerry B. Jenkins and Tim LaHaye, the authors of the series, are not suggesting that all people who have been left behind are evil and deserve their fates. Many of the characters accept Christ during their adventures and try to spread His word to their fellow survivors. The lesson here is that it is never too late to turn to Christ, even as the world is being destroyed.

Getting Right With God

Jenkins and LaHaye are not the first writers to dramatize those events; the end of the world has provided scenarios for books and movies for decades. Some of the stories had nothing to do with the final battle between good and evil, but instead were concocted by writers who wanted to alert people to the horrors of nuclear war.

The 1957 novel *On the Beach*, written by Nevil Shute, is a staple of many high school literature classes. It follows a submarine crew as they search for signs of life in a world that is slowly dying from the effects of fallout after a nuclear war.

With the collapse of the Soviet Union and the subsequent end of the Cold War in the early 1990s, nuclear annihilation became less of a threat. In recent years, it has been replaced by the fear of terrorism. On September 11, 2001, when Islamist terrorists hijacked airplanes and crashed them into the World Trade Center and Pentagon, causing some 3,000 deaths, interest in the coming Apocalypse greatly intensified.

"I would go for years without anyone asking about the End Times," a Presbyterian minister in New York named Thomas Tewell told *Time* magazine. "But since September 11, hard-core, crusty, cynical New York lawyers and stockbrokers who are not moved by anything are saying, 'Is the world going to end? Are all the events of the Bible coming true?' They want to get right with God. I've never seen anything like it in my 30 years in ministry." Other Christians wanted answers to their questions as well. Following the 2001 terrorist attacks, sales of the *Left Behind* books jumped 60 percent.

Belief in the Rapture

For young conservative Christians who are convinced the *Harry Potter* books promote witchcraft, or find slasher movies offensive because of their reliance on sexual themes and graphic violence, books and movies about the End Times may provide an opportunity to visit the supernatural in a safe way that promotes positive lessons about faith in God. "I like the *Left Behind* books because they are fun, exciting, easy to read and true," says

Major events, such as the September 11 terrorist attacks on the United States, cause some people to take a closer look at their faith and their belief in the End Times.

Abraham Lyle, a 12-year-old *Left Behind* fan who lives in Pennsylvania. "I also like them because they are Christian, and my parents like that I like them."

Some critics aren't sure the *Left Behind* books send the right message. Tina Pippin, a professor of religious studies at Agnes Scott College in Georgia, said in an interview with the *Philadelphia Inquirer* that the *Left Behind* books are "dangerous" and "they tap into a certain kind of American political ideology that thrives on crisis and distrusts global solutions. They express a perverse, pornographic desire that the world be destroyed. For some readers, the books are just fluff, adventure tales, good reading. But for believers, they represent a deep desire for the end of time."

The Gallup Youth Survey confirms that young people are certainly thinking hard about the End Times. A 2000 Gallup Youth Survey of 500 young people between the ages of 13 and 17 found that 81 percent of the respondents agreed with the statement, "There will be a day when God judges whether you go to heaven or hell." Many of those teens also believe in the Rapture, in which true followers of Jesus Christ will be awarded a place in heaven. Only 48 percent of the respondents said they could agree with the statement, "If you are a good person you will go to heaven, whether or not you believe in God." In another survey of 518 young people taken in 1994, 34 percent said they believe the world will end because of "a supernatural force, such as God's will."

The Millennium Bug

Over the years, many people who study Biblical prophecies have not only concluded the world will end but have actually predicted the date of the Apocalypse. Those predictions became

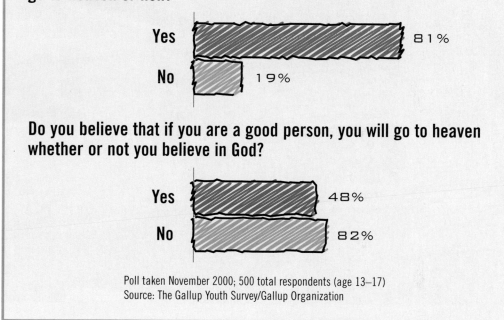

Do you believe there will be a day when God judges whether you will go to heaven or hell?

Yes — 81%

No — 19%

Do you believe that if you are a good person, you will go to heaven whether or not you believe in God?

Yes — 48%

No — 82%

Poll taken November 2000; 500 total respondents (age 13–17)
Source: The Gallup Youth Survey/Gallup Organization

quite common during the late 1990s, the years leading up to the new *millennium*. In 1994, for example, California-based Christian broadcaster Harold Camping announced that he had deduced the world would end that year sometime between September 6 and September 27. Camping said he based his prediction on some 30 years of studying the prophecies of the Bible. Obviously, he was wrong.

By 1999, a lot of people were worrying about the "Millennium Bug." For years, experts worried that many computers would fail to recognize the year 2000 as a legitimate date, and that this would

Before December 31, 1999, many Americans feared that chaos would result from widespread failure of computer systems because of the so-called "millennium bug." Some entrepreneurs sold emergency supply kits, containing food, water, and other necessary items, should the worst occur.

cause them to crash or have systemwide problems on January 1, 2000. Because governments, businesses, banks, and other organizations keep most of their records in computer files, some experts predicted mass chaos when every computer in the world locked up at the same time.

A poll conducted in 1999 by *Time* and CNN found that 59 percent of the respondents believed the Millennium Bug would cause computers to fail, 53 percent believed the world's banks would be disrupted, 38 percent said the turmoil caused by the bug would result in widespread rioting, and 9 percent believed "The world as we know it will end."

For months, people fearing the worst purchased gasoline-powered generators and stockpiled food, water, and other supplies in their homes, believing that the Millennium Bug would interfere with their ability to obtain the basic necessities. As it turned out, computers didn't crash and no one was forced to live off their stored supplies.

Continued Strong Interest in the End Times

People may have survived the Millennium Bug, but that does not mean they have stopped believing in the Apocalypse. When the final novel in the *Left Behind* series, *Glorious Appearing: The End of Days*, appeared in bookstores in the spring of 2004, it shot immediately to the top of the bestseller lists, even though critics generally panned its literary content. Jeff Guinn, books editor of the *Fort Worth Star-Telegram*, wrote that *Left Behind* fans are "getting what they want—more of the theologically reassuring same, and the more the better. For everyone else, it's a matter of the more, the tedious." Those are hardly words of praise, but *Left Behind* fans still flocked to bookstores to buy their copies.

There are plenty of other stories about the Apocalypse winding their way through popular culture. Among the Hollywood productions underway in 2004 were the feature film *The Fourth Beast: Mask of the Antichrist*, and *Revelations*, a six-hour TV miniseries. Both feature End Times dramatizations.

Video game fans are not being left behind either. When the video game *Diablo II* was released in 2000, it sold 184,000 copies in a single day and more than a million within the first month. In *Diablo II*, players will find an End Times scenario featuring plenty of action and lots of bloodshed as well as mystical creatures, magic potions, and evil winged villains. Other manufacturers have designed games around End Times scenarios as well. By the end of 2001, games with such titles as *Archangel* and *War in Heaven* were also available to young players. *War in Heaven*

THE END OF THE WORLD

The end of the world is inevitable, but if scientists are correct nobody has to worry about it for at least 6 billion years. That's when astronomers predict the sun will have converted all its hydrogen to helium, causing the exterior of the sun to expand and cool. That will turn the sun into a relatively large but cool star known as a red giant, which will envelope and devour the planets nearest to it—Mercury, Venus, and Earth.

Anybody living on Earth the day the last of the hydrogen is converted will likely see one final perfect sunrise. The yellow sun will shine brightly in the sky, then over a period of several million years the sun will slowly swell, heating the Earth. The polar ice caps will melt, flooding the Earth's land masses. Next, the seas will boil away and the atmosphere will burn off into space.

By now, the Earth and any life left on it would have been destroyed but the sun still has several million years to live. Next, the sun will burn up most of its helium, leaving mostly carbon and oxygen left in the interior. Those elements will continue to burn, causing the sun to expand and contract. What's left of the sun will eventually become a supernova and explode, shooting hot glowing material into space halfway to Pluto. An astronomer on a distant planet watching our sun is sure to notice, just as astronomers on Earth have witnessed other stars become supernovas.

Even after this catastrophe the sun is not quite dead. What's left of the sun after it goes supernova will be a small hot star known as a white dwarf. Surrounding the star will be a shell of colorful gasses, likely still containing fragments of the sun's former planets, including the Earth. Finally, the sun will cool quickly into a piece of dead dark matter known as a black dwarf.

enthusiasts found themselves dealing with such adversaries as winged demons as they trekked along the "Divine Path of Obedience" or the "Fallen Path of Power."

Manufacturers of the game said they definitely had a Christian audience in mind when they conceived the scenario for *War in Heaven*. "When you mention this is a Christian game, people assume there's no violence," Robert Westmoreland, an executive for the manufacturer of the game, said in a *New York Times* interview. "Sure, there's violence." Added the game's chief programmer, Andrew Lunstad, "Honestly, this is a spooky thing to be attempting in some ways. And let's face it, when you have angels fighting demons, it is going to be controversial. But I truly feel that God called me to do this."

Chapter Five

People dressed as aliens ride in the annual UFO Encounter parade through downtown Roswell, New Mexico. Roswell has been the center of UFO speculation in the United States since 1947, because of a strange crash that occurred in the desert near the town.

The Blurry Line Between Fiction and Fact

Life had mostly been a struggle for Norman Muscarello, but by the time the young man from Exeter, New Hampshire, turned 18 in 1965, he was looking forward to his future. After graduating from high school, Norman decided to join the U.S. Navy. His final few weeks in Exeter were busy as he prepared to leave for basic training. On September 2, just a few weeks before he was due to report for his induction, Norman drove his car to Amesbury, Massachusetts, where a friend had agreed to buy the vehicle. After dropping off the car, Norman had hoped to hitchhike the 12 miles back to Exeter, but traffic was light that evening and Norman ended up walking the entire way back. By 2 A.M., he still had a few miles to go. He was weary from the long walk and only wanted to get home and go to bed.

"I was thumbing down Route 50 towards Exeter, in Kensington near Mr. Dining's farm. It was a clear night, no rain," Norman recalled in an interview with an Exeter school newspaper years later. "There were plenty of stars in the sky. It was just a clear beautiful night." Suddenly, Norman saw something that made him freeze with fear. Here is how he described it to the Exeter student newspaper:

> I observed pulsating lights coming from the north, heading in a southwesterly direction, towards where I was. I assume the speed must have been something terrific because it came up on me all of a sudden . . . Very distant, pulsating erratically I couldn't make out any distinct pattern, circles or anything like that. It was just very bright. Could not make out a silhouette at all. I didn't know what it was. There was absolutely no sound, other than the fact that I heard horses in Dining's field, raising holy hell, kicking the barn. Crickets seemed to just quit . . . My attention was fixed on these lights. I didn't know what it was. Passed over, kind of like disappeared.
>
> I don't know what direction it went in. I was kind of dazed. My eyes were like, you know, seeing spots you go through when somebody takes your picture with a camera. Got my eyes cleared—son of a gun—here it comes again. I don't have to tell you, you get kind of nervous out there. I mean I'm all alone; there's nobody else standing there to refer to . . . I just froze up. I didn't know quite what to do. I got scared.
>
> I ran across the street. I didn't actually dive, I fell, because I tripped on something and I fell into the ditch, and I lay there with my head down. And I looked up . . . these lights were still pulsating in erratic positions. I couldn't make out any design or silhouette at all, and then it took off.

Norman ran all the way back to Exeter, where he reported what he saw to the police. Soon, newspaper and magazine journalists arrived in Exeter to report the story of the teenager who saw the unidentified flying object, or UFO. The air force also sent an investigator to interview Norman. As for Norman, he became a celebrity for a short time, but then the excitement over the UFO died down. He entered the navy, served in the Vietnam War, and went on to lead a quiet life in California and eventually back in New England before he died in 2003.

Norman gave the interview to the student newspaper in 1980— 15 years after he saw the UFO. In the intervening years, there had been many other UFO sightings, some even more bizarre than the one Norman described. During that period government agencies, congressional committees, and privately funded foundations explored the question of UFOs. All of them drew a similar conclusion—there is no verifiable scientific evidence that would prove the existence of flying saucers.

However, their conclusions could not shake Norman Muscarello's belief in what he claimed to have seen. "My personal opinion is—how naive and ignorant do we have to be to stand here and say that we are the only intelligent beings in this entire galaxy, solar system, and cosmos?" he told the student newspaper. "I don't believe that we are. It is something. I can't say it wasn't. I don't know what it was."

Ancient Astronauts?

Some UFO experts argue that encounters with *extraterrestrial* beings date back to the earliest days of civilization on Earth. They point to cave drawings they have interpreted as crude renderings of ancient astronauts. Or they point to such early architectural masterpieces as the pyramids in Egypt, and suggest that ordinary men of the era were incapable of designing or building such impressive structures. Men must have gotten help, they argue—perhaps alien visitors arrived and showed the Egyptians how to build the pyramids.

Nevertheless, it was not until June 24, 1947, when UFO mania really hit the public consciousness in the United States. That's when Kenneth Arnold, the pilot of a small plane, reported seeing nine UFOs streaking across the sky while he flew past Mount Rainier in Washington state. After landing his plane in Oregon, Arnold went to a local newspaper office to report his sighting. The newspaper published a story about Arnold's experience. That day, 20 people

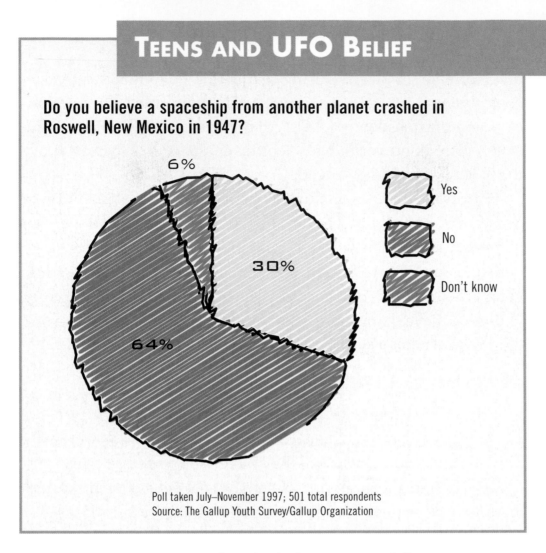

Teens and UFO Belief

Do you believe a spaceship from another planet crashed in Roswell, New Mexico in 1947?

6%

30%

64%

Yes

No

Don't know

Poll taken July–November 1997; 501 total respondents
Source: The Gallup Youth Survey/Gallup Organization

called the paper to report they had also witnessed flying saucers.

Two weeks after Arnold's encounter hit the newspapers, the *Roswell Daily Record* in Roswell, New Mexico, carried a similar story. On July 3, the newspaper reported, a ranch foreman named Mac Brazel had been out riding when he suddenly came upon the wreckage of what he thought had been an airplane. Brazel scooped up some of the debris and, a few days later, showed it to the local sheriff, who in turn contacted the nearby air force base. Soon, the story leaked out and the *Daily Record* reported that the military had found a flying saucer on the ranch.

Over much of the next six decades, the U.S. Air Force would find itself spending a considerable amount of time and resources sticking to its explanation that a flying saucer did not crash near Roswell and that all Mac Brazel found was probably the remnants of a weather balloon. Nevertheless, UFO enthusiasts have insisted that the Air Force has undertaken a massive cover-up, hiding evidence that a UFO crashed and that the government recovered the bodies of dead extraterrestrials. The assumption that aliens crash-landed near Roswell, New Mexico, has become the basis for many books, movies, and television shows. From 1999 until 2002, for example, one of the most popular TV shows on the WB network was *Roswell*, which told the story of teenage aliens trying to masquerade as, well, teenage Earthlings.

Political Messages

Science fiction stories were a staple of the entertainment industry long before Kenneth Arnold and Mac Brazel had their close encounters. During the 1930s, for example, moviegoers were usually treated to a chapter in the Buck Rogers or Flash Gordon space adventure serials before the main feature. On Halloween night in 1938, a radio dramatization of the H.G. Wells book *War of the Worlds* made it seem as though Martians bent on conquest were really invading the Earth. Although the narrator announced several times during the broadcast that the story was fabricated, many listeners believed the Earth was truly under attack by Martians. Newspapers reported many stories of people taking up arms and searching the countryside for invaders from space.

By the 1950s, many UFO stories were carrying subtle messages. The 1951 movie *The Thing from Another World* told the story of scientists in an Arctic Circle outpost fighting off a vampire-like vegetable man whose flying saucer crash lands near their base. They ultimately defeat the visitor, but the film ends with a warning to the audience to keep watching the sky. The message was for people to be wary of invaders — whether they were vampires from another planet or communists from the Soviet Union. A much more direct message was delivered in the 1951 movie *The Day the Earth Stood Still*, which ended with the extraterrestrial visitor warning Earthlings about the dangers of nuclear weapons.

Subsequent movies about UFOs and space travel seemed to contain fewer political messages. Instead, filmmakers concentrated on honing the special effects. In 1977, the first film in the Star Wars series was released. Young movie fans flocked to the epic science-fiction adventure. Respondents to a Gallup Youth Survey in 1979 voted *Star Wars: A New Hope* the "best movie ever"; in 1983 Gallup Youth Survey respondents chose the third installment in the series, *Return of the Jedi*, as their favorite movie of the year.

In the meantime, various congressional panels, government agencies, and private foundations examined the evidence connected to UFO sightings. They all concluded that flying saucer stories are false. From 1952 until 1969, the U.S. Air Force maintained Project Blue Book, which examined each sighting brought to its attention. During that time, the Air Force investigated some 12,000 UFO reports, and in all but 200 of the cases offered a plausible explanation for what might have prompted the witnesses to believe they saw flying saucers. In most cases, the air force suggested the witnesses had actually seen common aircraft, or bright celestial objects such as planets or meteors, or swamp gasses, or dozens of other natural occurrences. Finally, the U.S. Air Force decided to close down Project Blue Book, concluding that it had better things to do than chase flying saucer stories. Still, about 200 Project Blue Book cases remain unsolved, a fact that has given UFO enthusiasts grist for believing those sightings truly were close encounters with aliens.

Another investigation of UFOs was conducted under the leadership of physicist Edward U. Condon. Funded by the U.S. Department of Defense, the Condon Committee met for three

Yoda and other alien characters in science-fiction movies have shaped peoples' perceptions of what visitors from another planet might be like.

years, finally issuing a 1,000-page report in 1969. The committee decided that UFOs did not exist, stating, "Our general conclusion is that nothing has come from the study of UFOs in the past 21 years that has added to scientific knowledge." Since the Condon

ALBERT EINSTEIN AND THE TRUTH ABOUT SPACE TRAVEL

The United States first sent astronauts into space in 1961, and since then the nation has maintained a space exploration program. Essentially, though, the U.S. space program has hardly left its neighborhood. Astronauts have ventured no further than the moon; unmanned spacecraft have successfully landed on Mars and Venus, while others have carried out fly-by missions of more distant planets.

Is interstellar space travel possible? According to Albert Einstein, the answer is no. To begin with, one needs to comprehend the enormous distances separating the stars and how such distances are measured. The nearest star to our sun is Proxima Centauri in the constellation Centaurus. That star is four light years from Earth. A light year is the distance traveled by light in a year. Because light travels at 186,000 miles per second, a light year spans nearly 6 trillion miles. Therefore, it takes four years for the light from Proxima Centauri to travel across the vast gulf of space before it reaches the eyes of people on Earth. Another way of looking at it is for an observer on Earth to gaze at the star tonight. The light he would see actually left Proxima Centauri four years ago.

If it takes light from that star four years to reach Earth, how long would it take a spacecraft to travel the same distance? For a rocket to escape Earth's gravity, it must travel at more than 25,000 miles per hour. Point that rocket toward Proxima Centauri and the trip would take almost a million years. Obviously, the rocket would never have enough fuel to make the trip, and the pilot on board would be long dead by the time his plane arrived.

So the solution is to make the jet fly faster than light. Any science fiction movie fan has undoubtedly seen the captain of a spacecraft order the

Committee report was issued, the government has essentially dropped out of the UFO hunting business.

The SETI Project

The government has, however, assisted in the Search for Extraterrestrial Intelligence (SETI) project. The project attempts to

crew to accelerate into "light speed." And, if one would believe the UFO enthusiasts, that's how flying saucers cover the distance from star to star. But traveling at light speed is impossible, according to Einstein. In 1905, Einstein developed the Special Theory of Relativity, which concluded that it is impossible for an object to travel at the speed of light or faster.

First, Einstein determined that the speed of light is uniform and can't be added to the speed of a body in motion. In other words, the light emanating from a bicycle coasting down the street at 20 miles per hour travels at the speed of light, not the speed of light plus 20 miles per hour.

Next, Einstein pointed out that for an object to travel at the speed of light, it would have to depart from a stationary point of reference in order to achieve that speed. That can't happen, because Einstein proved that there is absolutely no stationary frame of reference in the universe. Everything in the universe—every planet, moon, asteroid, comet, and star—is constantly in motion. The Earth, for example, rotates on its axis and orbits the sun, which in turn is flying through space. The motion of the Earth, as well as every other object in the universe, is relative to one another. Therefore, light emanates from every object in the universe at the same speed and it is impossible for light from one object to overtake and pass light from another object.

Finally, Einstein concluded that the mass of a moving object increases with its speed. In speeds of just a few thousand miles an hour, the increase in mass—essentially, the size and weight of an object—isn't enough to notice. But at the speed of light, Einstein said an object's mass would grow to infinite proportions, proving that it is impossible for an object to obtain the speed of light.

TEENS AND EXTRATERRESTRIAL BEINGS

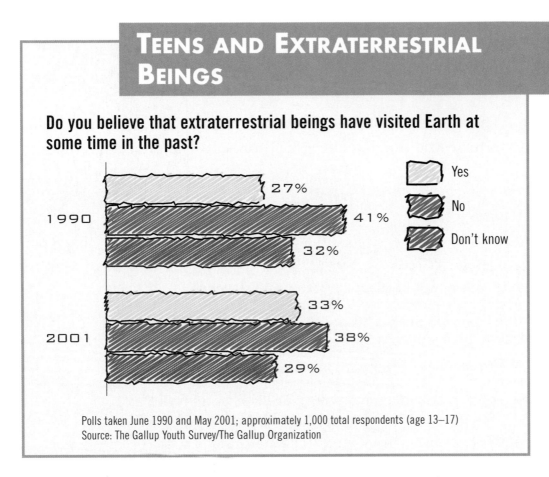

Do you believe that extraterrestrial beings have visited Earth at some time in the past?

Yes

No

Don't know

1990
27%
41%
32%

2001
33%
38%
29%

Polls taken June 1990 and May 2001; approximately 1,000 total respondents (age 13–17)
Source: The Gallup Youth Survey/The Gallup Organization

use scientific methods to search for life elsewhere in the universe. Most of SETI's efforts have been directed toward the operation of radio telescopes, which search for radio waves emanating from other stars. Most people think of telescopes as optical instruments, but a branch of *astronomy* is devoted to studying stars through the electronic radio waves they emit. To the human ear, these radio waves sound like static, but astronomers can learn a lot about a star's age, motions, and composition by studying its radio waves. Typically, radio telescopes are shaped like very large bowls or disks and can be pointed wherever the astronomer wishes, just as an optical telescope can be repositioned.

If a radio telescope can be used to study radio wavelengths of the stars, why can't it be used to listen for evidence of forms of life? That's mostly what the SETI project seeks to do. The U.S. government, through the National Aeronautics and Space Administration (NASA), operated a SETI program from the early 1970s until 1994, but then Congress cut funding due to a budget crunch. A private foundation, the California-based SETI Institute, now conducts the project, raising money for research through private donations. Occasionally, the SETI Institute has received government grants from NASA and the National Science Foundation.

Belief in UFOs

Just because the government doesn't believe in UFOs doesn't mean the American people have given up on the idea. That is particularly true for young people. Over the years, the Gallup Youth Survey has asked teenagers many times whether they believe in UFOs, and many have reported that they do harbor a belief in extraterrestrial visitors.

In 1978, for example, the Gallup Youth Survey estimated that 3.5 million teenagers not only believe in UFOs, but have actually seen unidentified flying objects for themselves. Fourteen percent of young people between the ages of 13 and 18 responded in a Gallup Youth Survey that they had witnessed what they thought was a UFO. In addition, 65 percent of the respondents said they believed in human-like life on other planets, while 61 percent of the respondents said they believe UFOs are "real." A total of 1,174 young people responded to the poll.

Twenty years later, in 1998, the Gallup Youth Survey again asked 500 young people about their feelings regarding extraterrestrial visitors. The poll found that 30 percent of teenagers believe a spacecraft landed in Roswell, New Mexico. One thing that is interesting about the poll is that it was conducted a year before the teen-oriented drama *Roswell* started airing on network TV. It means that young people were obviously following stories about UFOs on their own.

Crop Circles

UFOs have, of course, remained in the news over the years. These days a UFO sighting is generally met with skepticism and the media hardly flocks to interview witnesses. Still, developments in the UFO story do make it into the news from time to time.

For example, every so often a story appears in a newspaper reporting the appearance of crop circles. Usually, the circles are carved into an unsuspecting farmer's field, creating interesting and often intricate geometric patterns that UFO enthusiasts maintain are really efforts by extraterrestrials to communicate with us or, perhaps, with other extraterrestrials who may be searching for a place to land. Law enforcement officers usually blame Earth-bound pranksters. They argue that a homemade crop circle can be made by driving a stake into the ground, then attaching a rope to the stake. By holding onto the rope and walking in ever-increasing circles, skeptics claim it is possible for a prankster to mow down a sizeable number of corn stalks while making it appear to be the work of extraterrestrials.

In July 2003 a series of crop circles was found in a wheat field near Woodland, California. The largest circle was some 140 feet in diameter. Farmer Larry Balestra was asked by a CNN reporter whether he believed the crop circles were made by an extraterrestrial visitor. He answered: "It could be—I mean, we're not the only ones here in this universe. I don't think it's a UFO, but . . ."

And claims of government cover-ups didn't end with the Rosewell case. Twenty former employees of federal agencies—many of them one-time military workers—called a press conference in 2001 to demand new congressional hearings into the existence of UFOs. They claimed that the government had been involved in a cover-up of UFO evidence for some 50 years. In 2003, executives of the Sci Fi Channel, a cable television network that broadcasts science fiction programming, announced the hiring of a Washington lobbyist to help convince members of Congress to reopen UFO investigations. Officials from the network said they would push for a congressional hearing into UFOs because they believe the public wants one. They pointed out that a Sci Fi Channel documentary on the Roswell case drew an audience of 2.4 million people—more than double the network's normal viewing audience. "Our main goal is not to find a UFO," Sci Fi Channel Vice President Thomas Vitale told the Associated Press. "The goal is finding the truth. We're expanding and exploring the blurry line between what is science fiction and what is science fact."

Chapter Six

Many people believe that they have been visited or helped by angels. These supernatural creatures are considered superior to man in power and intelligence, and are often believed to be sent by God to help people on Earth cope with problems.

God's Messengers

Fourteen-year-old Timothy Keller of Norfolk, Virginia, should have been old enough to know not to play with guns. Still, during some horseplay with a loaded weapon, the gun discharged and Timothy sustained a bullet wound to his stomach. When Timothy's parents, Thomas and MaryAnna Keller, arrived at the hospital, they found their son laid out on an operating table being prepped for surgery. He was in a coma and near death.

Timothy spent six hours in surgery. Doctors successfully removed the bullet, but Timothy was not out of danger. For three days, the boy remained in critical condition. He ran a fever, which spiked as high as 105°F. He was also having trouble breathing, and a respirator tube had to be inserted into a lung. Thomas and MaryAnna Keller were told by Timothy's surgeons that nothing else could be done for their son, and that they should prepare themselves for the worst.

Thomas Keller, an ordained minister, never left Timothy's bedside during the ordeal. With Timothy's condition out of the hands of the doctors, Thomas Keller turned instead to the angel Raphael, whom the Bible says was entrusted by God with healing the sick. "As Tim lay in a coma, I cried out for help," Keller said in a story published in *Good Housekeeping* magazine. "I called on Raphael, the angel of healing, to save my son. And instantly, this huge, voluminous figure materialized in the room and I felt a sense of calm and love. The figure wore a flowing white satin robe with reddish trim. Although he didn't speak, and I couldn't see his face, I knew he was a masculine presence—Raphael. He hovered over the room, and I asked if he would just touch his bare foot to Timothy's chest. I somehow felt his touch would heal my son. Raphael complied—and then disappeared into thin air."

Within an hour, Timothy came out of his coma. His fever was gone. He could breathe without the assistance of a respirator. A day after Raphael's visit, the doctors pronounced Timothy out of danger. He was soon discharged from the hospital. Thomas Keller says there is no doubt who was responsible for his son's recovery. "Angels are all around us, willing to help," he says. "We only need ask that they touch our minds and hearts, and they will appear. Timothy is living proof."

Did an angel intercede in the life of Timothy Keller? Certainly, his father's description of the angel Raphael is not unique; others who claim to have seen or heard angels describe them as larger-than-life luminous figures who float silently through the air, hang around long enough to perform a miracle, then disappear as quickly as they arrive. Still, other people who claim to have seen angels describe them as coming in all shapes and sizes. Cancer patient Ann Cannady told *Time* in 1993 that she was visited by a tall, dark-skinned African-American man who knocked on her door one day and announced to a stunned Cannady and her husband that her cancer was in remission. "I am Thomas," he told her. "I am sent by God." Later, a hospital test confirmed what Thomas told Cannady: her cancer was gone.

Or, consider the case of 14-year-old Marilynn Webber of Wheaton, Illinois. After learning her Sunday school teacher was ill with cancer, Marilynn walked home in despair, not paying much attention to the world around her. In her daze, Marilynn had no idea that she had stepped in front of a railroad train until she chanced to look up and see the locomotive barreling down on her, so close she could see the terrified look on the face of the engineer. The train was too close to stop and Marilynn was too paralyzed with fear to jump out of the way. Suddenly, she felt a push. Evidently, somebody had bravely rushed up behind Marilynn and shoved her out of the way, just as the train arrived. "It was as if a giant pushed me from behind," Marilynn recalled in an interview with *Ladies Home Journal.* "I went flying off the tracks and fell down on the cinders just beyond."

Marilynn was anxious to thank the person who saved her life, so she waited by the tracks as the train passed. When the final car rushed by her, Marilynn looked across the tracks—and saw no one. In Marilynn's case, her angel was invisible. To Marilynn, there was no doubt in her mind who pushed her out of the way of the train. "My guardian angel saved my life," Marilynn said. "Who else could it have been?"

Angels Through the Ages

Many people assume that angels are creatures found only in Christianity, but that is not correct. The ancient Greeks believed in

Angel figures are used to decorate the roof of this ornate Christian church. Followers of other religions, such as Judaism and Islam, also believe in the existence of angels.

angels; the word is derived from the Greek word *angelos*, which means messenger. The ancient Jewish people also believed in angels. In the story of Passover, the holiday that celebrates the deliverance of the Hebrews from Egyptian slavery, God dispatched the angel of death to carry out the 10th plague, the slaying of the first-born children in each Egyptian home. Jewish families spared their children from the plague by smearing blood from lambs across their doors; that is how the angel of death knew to pass over their homes.

Muslims also believe in angels. It was the angel Gabriel who recited the book of Islamic laws known as the Qur'an to the prophet Muhammad. Other Islamic angels are said to record prayers in mosques and testify for or against people before they are permitted to enter heaven. Angels show up in dozens of other faiths, including Buddhism and Hinduism. Near the Euphrates River in Iraq, 4,000-year-old stone tablets have been unearthed depicting winged figures descending from the heavens.

In Christianity, it was Gabriel who brought Mary the message that she would bear a son named Jesus. Indeed, there are dozens of references to angels that appear throughout the New Testament. Matthew 16: 27 says, "For the Son of Man will come in the glory of His Father with His angels, and then He will reward each according to his works." St. John the *Evangelist* said, "And I beheld and I heard the voice of many angels round about the throne, and the number of them was thousands and thousands." Actually, there may even be more than St. John reported. Over the centuries, *theologians* have calculated that there could be nearly 400 million angels.

During the Middle Ages, Biblical scholars concluded that angels act as intermediaries between men and God, carrying His message to Earth, doing His bidding, and performing His miracles. It was also during this period that artists started portraying angels with wings and often with glowing halos encircling their heads.

Not all angels wear halos. Satan, at one time the most important angel in heaven, fell from grace when he wanted to be worshipped by man. He masqueraded as a serpent and tricked Eve into disobeying God. John Milton's 17th-century poem *Paradise Lost* describes how Satan is cast out of heaven along with many lesser angels who follow him into evil. Those angels became demons.

"Better to reign in hell than serve in heaven," declares Satan.

Angels could inspire people to perform great deeds. In the 15th century, a 14-year-old girl named Jeanne from the French town of Domremy-la-Pucelle started hearing the voices of angels. When she was 16, the angels told her she must lead her people against English invaders. The girl, who became known as Joan of Arc, convinced the future French king Charles VII that she had been chosen by the angels to defend France. Charles placed her at the head of an army, which under her leadership liberated Orleans and other French towns from English control. Later, Joan was burned at the stake when a church council leveled the false charge that she worshipped Satan. In 1920, Joan was elevated to sainthood.

A popular fictional story more familiar to Americans, perhaps, is the story of George Bailey, the despondent loan officer portrayed by actor James Stewart in the 1946 movie *It's a Wonderful Life*. The film—a staple of the Christmas season—tells how George is driven to the brink of suicide, but at the last moment is saved by a guardian angel named Clarence. To show George what the world would be like without him, Clarence takes the suicidal man on a tour of the town, during which they learn that the world would be a poorer and unhappier place if George had never been born. Clarence convinces George to give life a second try, and George gratefully accepts his guardian angel's advice.

Comfort in a Cruel World

At the start of the Protestant Reformation in the 16th century, reformers like Martin Luther dismissed the role of the angels, arguing that God could work His miracles on Earth without the help of angels. Over the next few centuries, Protestant theologians would essentially ignore the question of the existence of angels.

That changed in 1975, when influential U.S. evangelist Billy Graham published a book titled *Angels: God's Secret Agents*. The book, which argued that a proper interpretation of the Scriptures had to speak to the role of the angels, immediately shot to the top of the bestseller lists, selling some 2.6 million copies.

Billy Graham's endorsement of angels arrived at a time when the United States seemed in need of comfort. Americans were still bitter over the Vietnam War of the 1960s and early 1970s, and the Watergate scandal that forced President Richard M. Nixon to resign in 1974. Over the next three decades the United States would face economic problems, attacks by Islamic fundamentalists, racism, drug abuse, AIDS, and other social ills. "These are desperate times," Boston College philosophy professor Peter Kreeft told *Time*.

Evangelist Billy Graham speaks to more than 50,000 people at a 2003 rally in San Diego. Graham's 1975 book changed what many Christians believed about angels.

"People seek supernatural solutions to their problems. We want to reassure ourselves of our spiritualism." Clearly, it was time for the angels to come to the rescue.

Over the years, the Gallup Youth Survey has examined young people's beliefs in angels and has consistently found that many teenagers do harbor a belief in God's messengers. In fact, the Gallup Youth Survey has found that belief among young people in angels has increased over the years. In 1978, a Gallup Youth Survey found that 64 percent of American young people believe in angels; by 1994, that number had grown to 76 percent. During that same period, young peoples' beliefs in other supernatural concepts, such as Big Foot, the Loch Ness Monster, clairvoyance, and extra-sensory perception, have declined.

In a poll of 502 young people between the ages of 13 and 17 conducted in 1992, the Gallup Youth Survey found that 80 percent of teenage girls believe in angels. Also, many Catholics and regular church attendees were likely to maintain beliefs in angels; according to the survey, 81 percent of Catholic teens and 82 percent of regular church attendees harbored beliefs in angels.

"Most people think of angels as benign, pleasant and helping," University of Wisconsin psychiatrist Richard Thurrell told *Newsweek*. "And it's nice to have comfort in a cruel world."

Desperate Mortals

Billy Graham's book started a wave of interest in angels. Soon, angel enthusiasts organized into groups, such as the New Jersey-based Angel-Watch Network, and the Colorado-based Angel Collectors Club of America, whose members fill their homes with all manner of angel-based artifacts. One member, Joyce Berg, told *Newsweek* that she owns more than 10,000 items that depict angels—everything from cookie jars to postage stamps. Berg delightfully shows off her home in Beloit, Wisconsin, to visitors—dressed, of course, in a silver robe, wings, and a halo. Angels, Berg told *Newsweek*, "give you a good feeling."

Meanwhile, other books about angels soared onto the bestseller lists, and bookstores found themselves devoting not only whole shelves to literature about angels, but sections of the stores to the topic. Among the bestsellers to hit the bookstores were Sophy Burnham's *A Book About Angels* and its sequel, *Angel Letters*; Joan Wester Anderson's *Where Angels Walk*; and Eileen Elias Freeman's *Touched by Angels*.

Believers could follow the exploits of several TV angels. First to hit the screen was *Highway to Heaven*, which aired on the NBC network from 1984 to 1989 and featured Michael Landon as angel Jonathan Smith. Each week, Jonathan found himself wrapped up in the lives of desperate mortals who needed his help to solve their dilemmas. Of more recent vintage was the very similar *Touched by an Angel*, which aired on the CBS network from 1994 to 2003. This time, angels Monica, Tess, and Andrew dispensed comfort to assorted unwed mothers, suicidal teenagers, terminally ill fathers, and others who needed angelic assistance to resolve their problems. Soon, the producers realized that many of the shows' viewers longed to have angels of their own to turn to. One viewer, a suicidal teenager, wrote to actress Roma Downey, who portrayed Monica, stating that she changed her mind about killing herself after watching a *Touched by an Angel* episode in which Monica helped AIDS patients through their ordeals. "When I saw the pain on your face at the thought of those girls dying, it suddenly occurred to me that it might matter to someone if I died," the teenager wrote, in a letter quoted by *People Weekly*.

In 2003 and 2004 the television networks turned away from shows about angels. Two teen-based dramas, *Joan of Arcadia* and *Wonderfalls*, featured young protagonists who spoke directly to the Almighty rather than to angels. In *Joan of Arcadia*, for example, God appears to high school student Joan Girardi in such guises as a little girl in a playground, a hunky guy in school, and a maintenance man in a cherry-picker truck. As for *Wonderfalls*, the show focuses on young Niagara Falls antiques store clerk Jaye Tyler, who hears the word of God through talking objects, such as the small statuettes for sale in her store. Both shows center on the efforts of the two young characters to help people and change their lives for the better. Producers of the dramas emphasize, however, that unlike *Touched by An Angel* and *Highway to Heaven*, the characters in their shows may be receiving advice from God, but they are still using their own talents and intelligence to wade through human problems on their own. "Even though Joan has guidance from God, nothing gets solved in her life because of it," *Joan of Arcadia* creator Barbara Hall told the Associated Press.

This trend in entertainment does not mean that young people's fascination with angels is on the decline. With the world immersed in armed conflict; with disease, drugs, poverty, and homelessness still a burden to many young people; and with pressures mounting on teenagers to do well in school so they can get into a good college, a conversation with an angel now and again probably is not that uncommon. Today, it is likely that growing numbers of young people will turn to the supernatural for a variety of reasons. Some will look toward Wicca and Paganism to guide them on their spiritual paths. Some will study the End Times as they seek answers regarding the fate of the world. Some believe in UFOs and are convinced that space flight to the stars is possible. And

TEEN ATTENDANCE AT RELIGIOUS SERVICES

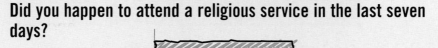

Did you happen to attend a religious service in the last seven days?

Yes — 43%
No — 57%

Did you take part in religious activities other than worship services, such as youth group meetings, religious classes, or choir rehearsals, in the last seven days?

Yes — 30%
No — 69%

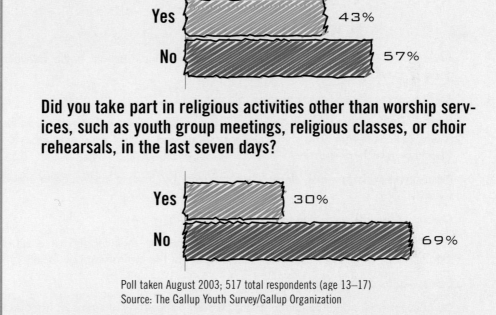

Poll taken August 2003; 517 total respondents (age 13–17)
Source: The Gallup Youth Survey/Gallup Organization

some merely enjoy reading about werewolves and vampires or going to horror movies because they love a good fright.

Filmmaker John Carpenter, director of the first of the *Halloween* slasher movies as well as several other occult thrillers, was asked recently by *Science Fiction Weekly* magazine to discuss his feelings about the paranormal. "I personally don't believe in the supernatural," Carpenter told the magazine. "On the movie screen, the supernatural certainly can exist, but in real life, no. But most people on the planet have a deep hunger for supernatural meaning. One can't just ignore it."

Glossary

APOCALYPSE—event marking the end of the world and ultimate battle between good and evil.

ASTRONOMY—scientific study of stars, planets, and other celestial objects.

ATTENTION DEFICIT DISORDER—believed to be caused by a chemical imbalance in the brain, ADD sufferers have short attention spans and exhibit impulsive behavior. Also known as hyperactivity.

BIPOLAR DISORDER—mental illness characterized by intense and sudden mood swings.

CHALICE—drinking cup, often used for ceremonial purposes.

CULTS—groups whose members are fiercely devoted to their leaders or a set of ideals, often religious in nature and existing out of the mainstream of society.

DEITIES—gods and goddesses.

DEPRESSION—emotional condition characterized by feelings of sadness, hopelessness and inadequacy.

EVANGELICAL—description of Christians who recognize their own sins and seek redemption through the acceptance of Jesus Christ as their savior.

EVANGELIST—preacher of the gospel.

EXTRATERRESTRIAL—a being that is not native to Earth.

FANTASY—fictional stories that involve mythical themes and characters, including dragons, ogres, wizards, and heroes with magical powers.

FOLKLORE—traditional beliefs, legends, and customs of a people.

GENRE—category of fiction or other artistic work.

HALLUCINATIONS—images, sounds, and other experiences of the senses that don't exist.

Glossary

INCENSE—gum residue from plants that when burned emits a sweet aroma; often used in religious services.

INQUISITION—period of European history spanning some 400 years in which religious officials used cruel methods, often involving torture, to investigate suspected cases of witchcraft and Satan worship.

LYCANTHROPY—mythical affliction that causes men to change into wolves.

MEDIEVAL—era in European history, spanning from about the year 500 to about 1500.

MILLENNIUM—period of 1,000 years.

OCCULT—lifestyle beyond the range of ordinary, usually shrouded in mystery and secret.

PARANORMAL—events or activities that occur beyond what is explainable through science or natural law.

PHOBIAS—obsessive or irrational fears.

PROPHECIES—predictions of the future, often made from a Biblical perspective.

PSYCHOSIS—mental illness that affects personality.

SCHIZOPHRENIA—mental illness that causes delusions or hallucinations, or causes the sufferer to have a distorted view of reality, a fragmented personality or expressions of other forms of bizarre behavior.

TAROT CARDS—set of 22 playing cards bearing mystical images, used to tell the future.

THEOLOGIANS—students of religion.

Internet Resources

http://www.gallup.com

Visitors to the Internet site maintained by The Gallup Organization can find results of Gallup Youth Surveys as well as many other research projects undertaken by the national polling firm.

http://www.stephenking.com

Fans of the horror writer can catch up with King's latest projects, read about his life, and download excerpts from some of his books. Many of the dozens of works cited on the Internet page include brief descriptions of the stories as well as information on when and how they were published.

http://www.parentstv.org

The Parents Television Council's ratings for every network television show broadcast in prime time can be accessed on the organization's Web site. Visitors will find "red," "yellow," and "green" alerts for each show, as well as news and position papers by the organization, which fights for family-oriented programming on TV.

http://www.tylwythteg.com/ufp.html#paganism

Visitors can learn about pagan traditions, history and legal rights at the World Wide Web site maintained by the Georgia-based federation. Member groups are listed as well as links and contact information. Visitors can also view plans for the federation's annual "Gathering of Tribes" at a campground along the Etowah River in Georgia north of Atlanta. Activities at the gathering often include workshops in holistic healing, meditation and use of herbs.

http://www.cog.org

The Berkeley-California based Wicca organization Covenant of the Goddess maintains an Internet page that features information about Wicca history and practices.

Internet Resources

http://www.leftbehind.com

Fans of the *Left Behind* books can find summaries, excerpts, and news of the series on the official World Wide Web page maintained by the publisher. Young readers can also send their e-mail comments to authors Tim LaHaye and Jerry B. Jenkins.

http://www.seacoastnh.com/arts/muscarello.html

Norman Muscarello's 1980 interview with students at Exeter Area High School in New Hampshire can be read at this Web address.

http://www.seti-inst.edu

Visitors to the Web page maintained by the California-based SETI Institute can learn about the organization's projects that search for intelligent life in the universe. The institute sponsors a weekly radio show, *Are We Alone?,* that is broadcast on 39 stations throughout the United States. For listeners who don't have access to the broadcasts, the institute has made available an on-line archive of the shows.

http://www.rickross.com

The New Jersey–based Rick A. Ross Institute maintains an extensive on-line archive of news stories about cults in the United States, particularly groups that are associated with occult themes.

http://www.witchway.net

Assorted rituals and spells practiced by pagans and Wiccans can be found at this Internet site.

Further Reading

Barrett, David V. Sects, 'Cults' and Alternative Religions: A World Survey and Sourcebook. London: Blandford, 1996.

Blum, Ralph, and Judy Blum. Beyond Earth: Man's Contact with UFOs. New York: Bantam Books, 1974.

Briggs, Constance. The Encyclopedia of Angels. New York: Plume, 1997.

Clark, Lynn Schofield. From Angels to Aliens: Teenagers, the Media, and the Supernatural. New York: Oxford University Press, 2003.

Elfman, Eric. Almanac of Alien Encounters. New York: Random House, 2001.

Enright, D.J. The Oxford Book of the Supernatural. New York: Oxford University Press, 1994.

Jones, Aphrodite. The Embrace: A True Vampire Story. New York: Pocket Books, 1999.

Jovanovic, Pierre. An Inquiry into the Existence of Guardian Angels. New York: M. Evans and Company, 1993.

King, Stephen. Danse Macabre. New York: Everest House, 1983.

LaHaye, Tim, and Jerry B. Jenkins. Are We Living in the End Times? Wheaton, Ill.: Tyndale House, 1999.

Leone, Bruce, ed. Paranormal Phenomena: Opposing Viewpoints. San Diego, Calif.: Greenhaven Press, 1997.

Sagan, Carl. Cosmos. New York: Random House, 1980.

Thompson, Kenneth. Angels and Aliens: UFOs and the Mythic Imagination. New York: Addison-Wesley, 1991.

Warner, John, and Margaret B. Warner. Aliens and UFOs: 21 Famous UFO Sightings. Providence, R.I.: Jamestown Publishers, 1994.

Index

Numbers in **bold italic** refer to captions and graphs.

Index

Index

Index

Picture Credits

Contributors

GEORGE GALLUP JR. is chairman of The George H. Gallup International Institute (sponsored by The Gallup International Research and Education Center, or GIREC) and is a senior scientist and member of the GIREC council. Mr. Gallup serves on many boards in the area of health, education, and religion.

Mr. Gallup is recognized internationally for his research and study on youth, health, religion, and urban problems. He has written numerous books including *My Kids On Drugs?* with Art Linkletter (Standard, 1981), *The Great American Success Story* with Alec Gallup and William Proctor (Dow Jones-Irwin, 1986), *Growing Up Scared in America* with Wendy Plump (Morehouse, 1995), *Surveying the Religious Landscape: Trends in U.S. Beliefs* with D. Michael Lindsay (Morehouse, 1999), and *The Next American Spirituality* with Timothy Jones (Chariot Victor Publishing, 1999).

Mr. Gallup received his BA degree from the Princeton University Department of Religion in 1954, and holds seven honorary degrees. He has received many awards, including the Charles E. Wilson Award in 1994, the Judge Issacs Lifetime Achievement Award in 1996, and the Bethune-DuBois Institute Award in 2000. Mr. Gallup lives near Princeton, New Jersey, with his wife, Kingsley. They have three grown children.

THE GALLUP YOUTH SURVEY was founded in 1977 by Dr. George Gallup to provide ongoing information on the opinions, beliefs and activities of America's high school students and to help society meet its responsibility to youth. The topics examined by the Gallup Youth Survey have covered a wide range—from abortion to zoology. From its founding through the year 2001, the Gallup Youth Survey sent more than 1,200 weekly reports to the Associated Press, to be distributed to newspapers around the nation. Since January 2002, Gallup Youth Survey reports have been made available on a weekly basis through the Gallup Tuesday Briefing.

HAL MARCOVITZ is a Pennsylvania-based journalist. He has written more than 50 books for young readers. His other titles for the Gallup Youth Survey series include *Teens and Cheating* and *Teens and Career Choices*. He lives in Chalfont, Pennsylvania, with his wife Gail and daughters Ashley and Michelle.